WOMEN FIND A WAY

THE MOVEMENT AND STORIES OF ROMAN CATHOLIC WOMENPRIESTS

BARBARA,

MAY THESE STORIES
BLESS & AFFIRM
YOU AS YOU ARE
GRACED ON THIS
SACRED FORMATION
OF LOVE & WILLINGNESS OF YES!
♡ MARY Ellen

"Women Find A Way," Edited by Elsie Hainz McGrath, Bridget Mary Meehan, Ida Raming.
ISBN 978-1-60264-223-2.
Published 2008 by Virtualbookworm.com Publishing Inc., P.O. Box 9949, College Station, TX
77842, US.
Manufactured in the United States of America.
Editors – USA:
Elsie Hainz McGrath
Bridget Mary Meehan
Editor – Europe:
Ida Raming
All proceeds from the sale of this book go to RCWP-International for the furthering of the
movement.
Visit us on the web at www.romancatholicwomenpriests.org.
Contact www.vitualbookworm.com for ordering information.
E-Book available at www.virtualbookworm.com.

CONTENTS

PREFACE

O N MAY 29, 2008, THE people of the world were further introduced to the "sins of the Fathers" as they attempted to decipher this official Vatican decree, published in that day's *Osservatore Romano*:

Congregation for the Doctrine of the Faith

General Decree

Regarding the crime of attempting sacred ordination of a woman

The Congregation for the Doctrine of the Faith, to protect the nature and validity of the sacrament of holy orders, in virtue of the special faculty conferred to it by the supreme authority of the Church (see canon 30, Canon Law), in the Ordinary Session of December 19, 2007, has decreed:

Remaining firm on what has been established by canon 1378 of the Canon Law, both he who has attempted to confer holy orders on a woman, and the woman who has attempted to receive the said sacrament, incurs in latae sententiae excommunication, reserved to the Apostolic See.

If he who has attempted to confer holy orders on a woman or if the woman who has attempted to receive holy orders, is a member of the faithful subject to the Code of Canon Law for the Eastern Churches, remaining firm on what has been established by canon 1443 of the same Code, they will be punished with major excommunication, whose remission remains reserved to the Apostolic See (see canon 1423, Canon Law of the Eastern Churches).

The current decree will come into immediate force from the moment of publication in the 'Osservatore Romano' and is absolute and universal.

William Cardinal Levada

Prefect

Angelo Amato, S.D.B.

Titular Archbishop of Sila

Secretary

1

Roman Catholic Womenpriests reject the penalty of excommunication issued by the Vatican Congregation for the Doctrine of Faith on May 29, 2008 stating that the "women priests and the bishops who ordain them would be excommunicated *latae sententiae*." We are loyal members of the church who stand in the prophetic tradition of holy obedience to the Spirit's call to change an unjust law that discriminates against women. We are obeying well-formed and well-informed consciences. We want no "winners and losers." We want no "fight." We want balance, a more holistic image of God, renewal. We want unity in a community of equals where all are welcome at the table. We want no more – and no less – than our brother Jesus wanted two thousand years ago. Our movement is receiving enthusiastic responses on the local, national and international level. We will continue to serve our beloved church in a renewed priestly ministry that welcomes all to celebrate the sacraments in inclusive, Christ-centered, Spirit-empowered communities wherever we are called.

The testimonies in this book are all from validly ordained Roman Catholic women. These are but a few of our stories. These are but a few of our priests. As you read the decree above, and then read the stories that follow, we invite you to remember the words of our non-Christian brother Mahatma Ghandi, as he prepared people to join him in prophetic obedience against unjust law [paraphrased]: "First they will ignore us. When that doesn't work, they will ridicule us. When that doesn't work, they will attack us. When that doesn't work, we win."

As Ghandi also reminded us, Christianity really has never been tried yet.

Will you support us in our efforts at trying it?

Elsie Hainz McGrath, Bridget Mary Meehan, Ida Raming

June 2, 2008

Dagmar Braun Celeste, Priest
Gisela Forster, Bishop
Christine Mayr-Lumetzberger, Bishop
Iris Müller, Priest
Ida Raming, Bishop

Ida Raming, left, with Iris Muller.   Christine Mayr-Lumetzberger

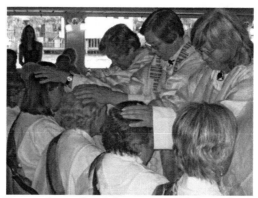

Bishop Gisela Forster is on far right, next to Bishop Ida Raming and
Bishop Patricia Fresen: Pittsburgh Ordinations, July 31, 2006.

SOLI DEO AMOR

Story of a Vagabond Troubadour
Dagmar Braun Celeste

F OR MANY YEARS I believed that the most important day of my
life was the day I was baptized. Then, after experiencing first
Communion, I was certain that no other day would ever match the
glory of that day. But in that same year even more grace was added on
the day of my confirmation. None of the elaborate trappings of that day
(dressed like a child bride) could camouflage the fact that I had become
co-responsible for the well-being of my Soul and the health of my
Church. That day I became a spiritual warrior, ready to lay down my
life for the love of God. Instead God simply gave me more blessings.
For over thirty years, I believed that nothing would ever overshadow
the radiant joy of my wedding day.

Little did I understand then that to become a bride and mother is to
embark on a *via dolorosa* The births of six children and later six
grandchildren were intensely grace-filled times, but not without thorns.
Then came the year of my divorce (insanity was less painful) and even
more excruciating, the day of my spouse's remarriage.

But Josephine's birth on St. Catherine's Feast Day brought relief
and joy back into my life, and my oldest daughter Gabriella's marriage
to Benjamin Cohen and the births of Emet and Eli, their sons, seemed
to tell me that all was well. After all the family tree is healthy and still
bearing fruit! Even the birth of Sam's (my spouse) seventh child, while
painful, was a sign of grace. And, miracle of miracles, Natalie's
marriage the year of my ordination and little Therese Dora's birth in
2006. Life simply keeps flowing like a river....

Looking back and remembering how far God has brought me and
looking ahead to where S/He wants me to follow fills me with gratitude
and awe and peaceful certainty that it is God's Spirit who is calling me
to sing this new song .

On February 28, 2002, everything began to change again, and now
I believe that the most important day of my life until forever will be

4

June 28, 2002, the day I decided to accept God's invitation to the priesthood. Back on that February day, in a phone call from Austria, the place of my birth, I was invited to join a small band of spiritual warrior women ready to claim ordination, *contra legem* if necessary. So the time had come to relinquish the driver's seat once and for all – to Jesus – and to accept him as my only Beloved and become willing to follow him back to the future. Even home to Austria if that is where he needs my valiant YES.

When Christine, the leader of the Austrian group, asserted back in 2000 that by the time her women, then in training, would be done with their formation, a Roman Catholic bishop would emerge willing to ordain them, I listened to her words and heard her hope, but I did not believe her. I should have known better. After all, by then I had lived for many years under the motto of the great state of Ohio: With God all things are possible. And so that February morning I was less inclined to doubt Christine's promise that not one but two Roman Catholic bishops were ready to ordain her women.

When I first met Christine I still had no awareness of my own call to ordination. Since the early 1970's, I had worked in the feminist vineyard, supporting an untold number of causes where women organized to empower each other personally, politically and spiritually and were struggling to set one another free, body, mind and soul.

I had gone to the first Women's Ordination Conference in Detroit, where my good friend Roberta and I seemed to be the only women in our section of the hall not called to ordination. I had been selected by Margaret Ellen Traxler's (3/12/1924—2/12/2002) Institute for Women Today as one of the most promising young women in the country. I did not then understand why. When she died, shortly after I got my phone call, I began to see what perhaps she saw, way back then, that I thirsted for justice in society and church. I was a risk-taker who was willing to cut to the heart of the matter and ready to live on the cutting edge, dreaming of things that never were and asking, "Why not?" Margaret was a mentor equal to Dr. Lotte Leitmeier, the first, and for years the only, female canon lawyer in the world – and my Latin and theology professor at the Neuland School in Vienna; and to Mother Teresa, an unknown sister whom I had the honor of volunteering for in New Delhi, India in the early 60's.

In a special spring newsletter from The National Coalition of American Nuns, her friends remembered Margaret's courage in confronting powers and principalities, from the Civil Rights March in Selma in the 60's all the way to the march across St. Peter's Square in

Rome in 1994. Together with members of NCAN, she unfurled a very large banner that said it all: They Are Meeting About Us Without Us! And guess what? Decades later, they still are.

But as grateful as I am to all the wonderful Catholic women who taught, empowered and directed me, I have to acknowledge that it was two Methodist women on Kelleys Island, Ohio, who first opened my eyes to the possibility of this call. A few years back, after I had finished a workshop for Sacred Space at Himmelblau House, our island family home, entitled The Mystery of the Blue Rose, first one and then a second woman came up to me and asked – since I had my Masters degree from Methesco (Methodist Theological School of Ohio) – whether I would be willing to consider becoming their pastor. At first I thought they were simply confused. Perhaps they did not know that I am Catholic? But God had a surprising lesson in store for me. They simply did not care!

When I returned to Cleveland, I made an appointment with Rev. Otis Moss, pastor of Olivet Baptist Church, and after some careful listening he handed me a wonderful book whose title said well what I was feeling then: *God's Yes Is Louder Than Your No.*

Still, I was not ready to yield the driver's seat yet. After much prayer and discussion with my spiritual director, I rejected the women's invitation. The price of excommunication seemed too steep a price and the exodus from my church appeared impossible. If I was to be ordained, I argued with God, then it had to come from the Roman Catholic Church. Nothing less than a Roman Catholic bishop would do.

So…God responded…with two.

Now what? How many more excuses could I drum up? Oh, you would be surprised! Almost daily I thought of them, and if I missed a day someone else would surely remind me that excommunication and exodus were still inevitable despite my determination to stay within the Church. But this time my spiritual director was more respectful of the call. She simply asked me to bring Fr. Hritz into the dialogue, and to talk to my family and friends, and to continue to pray for "freedom of heart." I did, and the heart theme followed me throughout my preparation and eventual ordination.

After I returned from Austria, I met with Bishop Pilla in Cleveland who, like many others, simply asked, "Now that you are ordained what can you do with it?" as if utility could embrace the full measure of the sacrament. I replied, "I suppose, since my church will neither test my call nor legitimate my ordination, I will be free to simply become more effective at doing what I am already doing." Help my daughter Noelle take care of Josephine and support other single women with children, especially addicted women transitioning out of prison; grow the TYRIAN network (founded July 25, 2000, the feast day of St. James) into whatever God wants it to become; be part of creating recovery opportunities for those addicted to sex and other mood altering substances; be of service in Ohio City where I was beginning to plan the building my Dream Catcher Hermitage right next door to Noelle and Josephine's home; help my friends create places of healing and opportunities for holiness, and continue to offer free polarity treatments to those who might benefit from them.

Chris Schenk, founder of FutureChurch and one of the Sisters of St. Joseph who for a short while was helping in this discernment process, said it best: "If this is God's will. nothing can stop it and if it is not God's will nothing can help it."

I do trust that Jesus Christ, whose mercy has sustained me thus far, will not desert me ever. And I do know that I am free to accept his invitation in good conscience but also free to reject it without dire consequences to my Soul. But I agree with Bishop Rafael and Christine that to live with the knowledge that I have chosen to be less than I am called to be would be a sad life. The price of saying YES might be exodus. But the price of saying NO might be a broken spirit added to my already broken heart.

I thank God for all for the truth, insight, prayers and clarity I have received from the Cleveland Carmelite community, especially through Sr. Pat's creativity and compassion and Sr. Anna Mae's courage and generosity. I am also especially grateful to Sr. Susan and the Humility of Mary community for offering me and Evelyn Hunt, my discernment companion, hospitality and acceptance throughout my discernment retreat.

When I asked my dear friend Sr. Ruthmary to give me a good question with which to walk the labyrinth at the Villa, she quietly suggested I simply ask to be shown the "path with heart." And so I did and what I found that day at the heart of the labyrinth was a six-petaled lotus which spoke to me of my six children and the love they represent: The love I feel for their father, for them and their children and spouses, and the love I treasure in my own motherly heart for them and all they are and will be called to be.

Without honoring God the Mother and all the female aspects of God there cannot be balance or healing for us women or our Church. This is why together with men of good will we must do whatever is possible to non-violently but valiantly gain new ground (Neuland) in our own churches. We must insist that women and men together can and will bring new life to the whole Catholic Church if each of us and all of us claim the freedom to follow Jesus Christ wherever he calls us to go (see *Pacem in terra*, Pope John XXIII).

In this light, excommunication may be as necessary on the path with heart as crucifixion was necessary on Jesus' *via dolorosa*.

Ordained a priest: 2002 Passau

THE START

The Danube Seven and the Bishop Heroes
Gisela Forster

ON THE 29TH OF June, 2002, seven women went on a ship on the Danube, in Passau, prepared to be ordained by a Roman Catholic bishop with apostolic succession.

For years before, they had met one another in monasteries and other special places, had lighted candles, hoped and wept, argued and wrung their hands. Their aim was clear: They all wanted to be ordained as women priests, they were well qualified to become priests, but the Vatican didn't allow women to be ordained. Therefore, the women had to begin the process on their own. When they were ready, they would be ordained by a valid male bishop, and so their ordinations would also be valid.

Three groups started: one in Linz, one in Innsbruck, and one in Vienna About thirty women, most of them theologians, teachers, religious sisters, or nurses, embarked on a long and intensive preparation program.

Once they met in a monastery near Passau. They sat the whole day in a circle and talked. In the building also was a group of women seamstresses. They often came to the priestly preparation group and asked them: "What are you doing? No clothes sewing? No painting of blouses or something? We see nothing!" The priestly women answered: "No, we have nothing to show you now, we are working for the future."

They knew: They were preparing a program and searching for a bishop who could ordain them. But how could they tell these others that?

I was one of these women, and I felt myself ready to work against the inequality of the Vatican. In my youth, I had loved church, loved the singing, the music, the art, the rituals. I would have liked to become an acolyte, but it was not allowed for girls. I saw the bigotry of the hierarchy – against females and against love – and I was shocked.

Later, I married a priest, had children, and gave up my cause because of his priesthood. I struggled in many support groups of women against celibacy and mothers of priest's children. I hoped things would change, but I saw more and more clearly that no pope who lives in fear of women, especially in fear of strong priestly women, would ever change the injustice. More and more, I saw the fight of the church hierarchy as a fight to show everybody that the space around the altar was off limits to women. We women would have to say, "We also are human beings, and men cannot forbid us to lead a parish, to work with the youth and to bless dying people.

It was a blessed group in which we worked. We were strong women with high qualifications and clear wishes.

Our dream became more and more real. We came up with the plan to be ordained on a ship, because nobody would give us space in a church: a ship as symbol of flowing water, as symbol of the ship of the church. We hired a ship in Passau, a little town between Bavaria and Austria. We told the ship's owners that there would be a ceremony on the boat, and they answered, "The Caritas always do the same." We smiled, because we were not the Caritas. Nevertheless, we were anxious that, if the truth were known, somebody would take the ship away from us, so we promised that nobody should know that the ordination should be on a ship.

The biggest problem was how to find a bishop with real apostolic succession. We searched the whole world. One who we thought would do it had recently died; another had not the courage.

A journalist from the ORF (Austrian TV) interviewed me, and I said we were determined to be ordained. I said it was time to give women the same rights that men have!

Some days later, my daughter told me that at six o'clock in the morning she had heard me on the radio. I thought it was a joke. Two hours later, journalists came to my school and asked me if it was true that I was to be ordained a priest. I said, "Yes, it is true, but I can tell you only the day and not the place." But the journalists would not stop asking me, so I told them I would give them a hypothetical example: "The bishop will come in a helicopter and will drop a robe down in a woods where the women are waiting. Then the bishop will throw holy water out from the helicopter and ordain us." I thought it was a funny story, but nobody had heard the word "example." The next day, every newspaper published the story of the helicopter.

Many people listened to us, but still we had no bishop.

Then, suddenly, we had two.

We had not been searching alone, as some priests had searched with us, and so we found two bishops from two different countries who were both convinced that it was necessary to ordain women.

So it was that on March 25th we had a lovely diaconate ordination in a private house in Austria. The ordained women were Dr. Ida Raming, Dr. Iris Müller, Dr. Gisela Forster, Christine Mayr-Lumetzberger, Viktoria Sperrer, and Adelinde Roitinger. The ceremony was moving, and the two bishops and we women are all absolutely certain of the ordination's validity.

One of the bishops, who was from a very faraway country, asked us if the priest Rafael Regelsberger could be our bishop here in Europe, and we agreed. So Rafael Regelsberger was ordained a bishop two months later, in May of 2002.

For the big priestly ordination, on the 29th of June, 2002, we invited both bishops and Bishop Rafael Regelsberger. There would be three ordaining bishops.

Before the day of the ordination arrived, members of the Roman Catholic Church threatened everybody who would be present at the ordination with excommunication, including journalists. But people did not accept this threat. They told everybody that they were sure they would not be excommunicated simply by being present at the ordination. Everyone wanted to be there, and many people tried to get on the ship.

Church personnel became very angry. They sued to rent the whole ship, but the owners told them they could rent the ship only if they paid more than we had paid. The case was finally closed on Friday afternoon and the bishop could not that quickly bring enough money to rent the ship, so the hierarchy was without success.

The ship stayed ours. The history continued.

On the morning of June 29th we went to the ship. On the side of the ship were persons who filmed everybody who came. Many came, but one of the bishops did not. Two were present. So the ship sailed with two bishops, and seven women ready to be ordained: Dr. Ida Raming, Dr. Iris Müller, Dr. Gisela Forster, Christine Mayr-Lumetzberger, Adelinde Roitinger, Dagmar Celeste, and Pia Brunner.

Later, the missing bishop told us that he had traveled to Passau and asked a community for overnight accommodations on the day before the ordination. During the night, his door was locked from the outside and he could not exit the room. The whole next day, the day of the ordinations, he was locked away by the Roman Catholic community.

It was a deeply moving ceremony for everybody on the ship, and especially for us women. During the prostration, I felt the earth under my body – the whole earth, which doesn't choose between men and women, but loves all and gives everyone ground.

The next day, when I returned to my work as a nurse, a patient of mine could not believe that the Vatican was not able to stop us. He asked: "What did they do to stop the ordination? Did they put a hole into the ship?" I said no. "Why not?" he said. "Are they not able to stop seven women?"

I answered, "No, they are not able to stop us, the Danube Seven."

Indeed, we were the victors. We were ordained, really and validly!

The Vatican hierarchy was more than angry: Very soon, they sent us the Decree of Excommunication. First came the Admonition, urging that we repent. We answered that we cannot repent being women.

My papers of excommunication lay under the entryway doormat where people clean their shoes. First I could not recognize the envelope. It seemed to be a letter from a winery because of the red words in the corner. Later I realized it was "Vatican red," not "wine red." The envelope didn't have a stamp, so I thought it was a common letter to every address, advertising church products. Still later, I noticed that the envelope didn't have a stamp because it had been delivered directly from the Papal Nuncio in Berlin to my house. The excommunication was printed on a very heavy and rich paper, and signed by twelve cardinals and Joseph Cardinal Ratzinger, later Pope Benedict, an early student and friend of my husband.

I was very sorry that the Vatican had excommunicated me. I wrote them that they should give me a chance to refute it, but they didn't give me that chance.

Three months later, I got a call from another bishop who said he wanted to meet me. He had seen me on television. We met, and I told him of the vision of us women: to bring priestly ordination to all women of the world who want to be ordained. He said he would support us. We concluded that women should not be ordained by male bishops who must hide their identities from the hierarchy. He said that he was ready to ordain me a bishop because women could ordain other women openly.

"No," I said, "not me, others perhaps." I asked Ida Raming if she wanted to be ordained a bishop, but she did not feel healthy at that time. I asked Christine Mayr-Lumetzberger. She felt ready. Ultimately, I was convinced also, and in the following months, Christine and I were ordained as bishops by three valid male bishops.

The ordaining ceremony was very dramatic. We met the bishop and then we drove in three cars to the church where the ordination would be done secretly. In the first car was our priest friend, in the second the bishop, and in the third Christine and me. We all kept the same speed, but suddenly a policeman stopped the car with the bishop. Our breath stopped too, because we thought that the Vatican had found us and would carry the bishop away. But it was not the Vatican, only a policeman. We didn't argue that we were all traveling at the same speed; we paid the fine and continued on our journey to the church. The notary controlled and noted our passports. Then we all went in, closed and locked the church door, and donned liturgical vestments. The bishop told us that these ordinations were not for us, but for bringing ordination to all women in the world who desire to become priests. And we heard him say: "Don't sleep, don't do 'nothing,' don't think this is enough. Be active as bishops, go to the people and to those who need you."

It was late in the night when we drove away, in all directions, to bring our hearts, our feelings, and our desires to the people of the world who have a big longing for equality and justice for women.

Many names of bishops have to remain secret because the Vatican is not ready to listen or talk to women, but those names are all noted by notaries, and the day will come when the documents will be opened and the Roman Catholic hierarchy will say, "Welcome! Welcome to all women priests and women bishops."

So I hope. May you hope with me.

Ordained a priest, 2002 Passau
Ordained a bishop, 2003 Austria

REFLECTIONS ON MY WAY

God's Call To Me
Christine Mayr-Lumetzberger

THROUGH ALL MY LIFE I had been feeling the call. My younger days were a long time of suppression of my call, because I was told that God would never call a girl to priesthood. But for myself I have never denied what I had experienced: a call to serve God by joining others on their way to God.

Over the course of decades, the ecclesiastical climate changed slightly. It was at the First European Women's Synod in Gmunden, Austria, in 1996, when I felt strong encouragement by many women talking about their priestly vocation openly and frankly. This experience was my personal kick-off for my active work on women's ordination.

At that time I was quite well informed about all the theoretical groundwork, which had been accomplished by a host of theologians, in particular by their feminist minority. Considering all that with proper respect, I myself have never felt forced to do theoretical work. I had the feeling that the groundwork on women in the church had reached a level on which a practical approach had to follow. I decided not to join into the discussion on women's ordination, but to do take a practical step by setting down facts.

As there were no legal possibilities at all to prepare oneself actively for priestly ministry, I started to develop a concept for a training course by myself. It was not only a question of humbleness but mainly of reason, to involve a great number of bright and willing people in this development process. In particular, the constructive participation of many priest friends showed that I had opened a valve to fill a huge vacuum.

The result of this three-year process was a "program for the preparation of women for sacramental orders in the Roman Catholic Church." In 1999, this program was approved unanimously and supported by the general assembly of We Are Church – Austria, and

14

the training program started in three groups under my leadership. In 2002, several of the participating women made the decision to strive for the priestly ordination together with me.

The initial situation was this: The goal was clear, but nobody knew the route, no bishop in sight. But my certainty was: "If God is really willing to have women priests, God will provide. We just have to keep the road clear." So we scheduled and organized the ordination and I took a hefty financial risk in renting the ship. It must have been God's help: Bishops came to us advising of their readiness to lay hands on us.

On My Understanding of Ministry

Throughout about 35 years of pastoral work I have been endeavoring to join men and women on their way to God. Saint Benedict has designated the "true search of God" as the most important mission of a monk. In this tradition, I have received my spiritual education and this is my way of comprehending my priestly and episcopal ministry. Of course, as an initiator and a "pathfinder", my ministry has also a prophetic dimension. I encourage women to rely on the help and the power of the Holy Spirit and to allow themselves to be guided by the Spirit on new paths.

An important part of my understanding of ministry is my civilian profession. As a working priest, I am trying to do my best in my job as a teacher, just like millions of other people do. And 27 years of marriage do not set me apart from many others. These offer me a mark of credibility as a priest within the community of the faithful.

The episcopal ministry of leadership makes very heavy demands on me. It is mainly the ministry for unity, reaching from simple liturgy to complex cooperation in the worldwide church. This requires that I scrutinize my goals and reorient myself to the gospel again and again. Jesus' question to Peter, "Do you love me?" is directed to all the priests and bishops – but first and foremost it is a question to me. Only if my episcopal performance is guided by my love for God, will I earn credibility among the faithful. According to the formula of St. Ignatius of Antioch, *ubi episcopus, ibi Ecclesia,* I have to take responsibility for a particular portion of the church. The church – considered as the body of Christ – consists of living members, women and men. In order to keep this body alive and healthy, I have to make an effort for a constructive togetherness of all bearers of responsibility. The Roman Catholic Church of the third millennium offers a very wide field of work.

Ever since hearing the call to priestly ministry, I have trusted in the guidance of the Holy Spirit, just like the Apostles Peter, Paul, Mary Magdalene and all the saints.

Responses To My Ministry

Throughout these years, people have to a large extent accepted my priestly ministries gladly. They contact me directly by e-mail or phone or through third parties. They ask for services and sacraments, but also for spiritual conversation and advice. But a great part of my priestly work has to be done in everyday situations: my hairdresser seizes the opportunity to talk with me, strangers come up to me in the queue before the cash desk of the supermarket and start a conversation, my colleagues in my job sometimes wait for a word of mine, and many a chat in a pub has turned into a real confession.

As I have always fostered good relationships in my contacts with brothers in priestly ministry, they all are very friendly and respectful to me now. I have many amicable relationships with priests and bishops. Together with them, I am working on future paths, which can be walked upon by priestly men and women – side by side.

A Political Act

To go our way *contra legem* was not at all a frivolous decision. I had been hesitating seriously and for a long time to affront or disappoint my friends and brothers in a way like this. I was not willing to tear up new rifts or to set up walls. I had a good basis of discussion with my local bishop at that time, and through him indirectly also with the Bishops Conference. I had been keeping him informed about the progress of my women's training program. Parts of my program were adopted by the seminaries for the men's training.

But in January 2002, we made our group decision to strive for ordination actively. According to the example set by the five wise virgins (Mt 25, 1-13) and with the certainty that if God is really willing to have women priests, God will provide ordaining bishops, I took the risk of a violation of the church law. Trusting in Divine Providence, I booked the ship. As the bishops had agreed to ordain us autonomously and of their own free will, I decided that the violation of the taboo was the one and only way to void an unjust paragraph of the Canon Law.

And it was not only an important experience, but also a strong encouragement for me, when a high church official expressed his surprise: "Oh, now I see you are not only talking about, but you are actually going to do something."

Also in civil law an unjust law will usually be changed only after it is violated. Subsequently the case may be administered newly and the law may be readjusted to the new facts. This procedure is also applicable to Canon Law. However, the Vatican needs much more time.

A Pioneering Situation

When I began to talk publicly about female vocation I experienced surprisingly great support from either side. But it was split into two parts: The goal of women priests in the Roman Catholic Church was generally agreed – even by ecclesiastical dignitaries – and the opponents were a small minority. But concerning the strategy to achieve this goal, the overwhelming majority of supporters and advisers knew precisely how it would NOT work. Again and again, I was urged to keep my hands off. There was not one single voice of encouragement, not to mention any constructive ideas. So I had to find a way by myself.

It was like the attempt to climb up a mountain of 25.000 feet for the first time. A very small group of supporting friends started out with me to search for a path to ordination.

We found a path and we set out. When this news got into the public, a few of our supporters dissociated themselves from the group, and some of them turned into opponents. It was a great disappointment to see that the headwind came mainly from the female side. All but a few of those women who were invited to be ordained side by side with us had withdrawn at the last moment.

But in this process, I also got to experience a new quality of steady friendship and loyalty. It was not always easy to keep pursuing the goal while far away from the certainty of the mainstream. But I found comfort and encouragement in the letters of St. Paul: "I have fought a good fight, I have finished the race, I have kept the faith." (2 Tim 4:7).

A Prophetic Act

A further consideration of mine was the "prophetic action." The choice was simple: either observe the Canon and refuse God's call, or follow the call by an ordination *contra legem*. Even though the ordination was not allowed within the scope of the church law, it was valid according to the intentions of the ordaining bishops and the ordinands and the rite prescribed.

For many decades women have yearned for ordination and struggled for it, but no one dared to actually take this step. By my ordination I also wanted to encourage the many women – and men as

17

well – to follow God's call to priestly ministry. Moreover, I wanted to show the legislators of the church that the Holy Spirit is acting in the church by persuading bishops to ordain women and persuading women to receive ordination.

As is usual in the Benedictine tradition, I would like to close with the acronym U.I.O.G.D., *ut in omnibus glorificetur Deus* – that God may be glorified in all things.

Ordained a priest: 2002 on the River Danube near Passau
Ordained a bishop, 2003 Austria

MY STORY, CONDENSED

Iris Müller

I WAS BORN IN 1930 in Magdeburg in mid-eastern Germany. After my final high school examination in 1950, I studied Protestant theology at the Cathechetical Major Seminary in Naumburg/Halle. In 1955, I continued my theological studies at the Martin Luther University in Halle/Saale, and received a diploma in theology in 1958. After this examination, which qualified me to serve as a pastor in the Protestant Church, I converted to the Roman Catholic Church – a church that I found expressed its following of Christ not just in words but in full sacramental reality, a community of faith that truly spanned the whole world.

The consequences of that religious decision were extremely difficult. As a woman, I now came under the restrictions of Catholic Canon Law. I had become a creature incapable of receiving Holy Orders (cf. c. 1024 CIC). I was expected to renounce my wish to be ordained as a woman. My Catholic community, both priests and lay people, wanted me to consider my call to the priesthood meaningless. I was expected to accept the status quo and worth of women in the Catholic Church.

A further consequence of my conversion was that there was no prospect of employment for me as a Catholic theologian in the communist regime of the DDR (East German Republic) because I refused to become a member of the communist party SED. My situation became so critical that I had to leave the DDR illegally. I found refuge in West Germany (BRD) in 1959.

After many problems, I succeeded in continuing my theological studies with the faculty of Catholic theology in Münster. As in the DDR, my Catholic surroundings, the professors and most of the students, expected me to simply accept the position of women in the Church without further question. But I decided to be faithful to my conviction, and to my call to ordination. So, as a former Protestant theologian, I was the first woman in the Catholic faculty to give witness that women were discriminated against in the Catholic Church and that their inferior status had to be reformed. On my pioneering path for women's equality and women's ordination, I found solidarity and support from Ida Raming, a student at the same faculty. In 1963, during Vatican Council II, we together wrote a petition to the Council calling for women's ordination.

In 1970, I completed my doctorate in theology. During the following years, I remained a member of the faculty in Münster as a scientific assistant. I was involved in building up a special library on the status of women in the three monotheistic religions (Judaism, Christianity and Islam). It was titled "Women in Religion."

After a lifetime struggle for women's equality and women's ordination in the Catholic Church, I decided to follow my call to the priesthood. Together with my friend and colleague, Ida Raming, I was ordained a priest in 2002. My heartfelt wish is that our movement, Roman Catholic Womenpriests, will continue to grow and flourish, and that it will open the door to full freedom and equality for women in the Roman Catholic Church.

Ordained a priest: 2002 Passau

SITUATION OF WOMEN IN THE ROMAN CATHOLIC CHURCH

Canonical Background and Perspective
Ida Raming

The present status of women according to CIC/1983 and according to the Magisterium

M ORE THAN HALF OF THE MEMBERS of the Roman Catholic Church are women; yet the public appearance of this church is that of a man's church. Only men hold the positions and offices of decision-making within this community. They decide on the doctrines of faith, the moral principles and the laws of the church, without any participation by women.

How did this apparently strange structure of the Roman Catholic Church come into being, compared to the democratic structure of civilized states with their principles of human rights and equality for men and women?

Fundamental to the answer is canon law CIC c. 1024: "Only a baptised man can validly receive sacred ordination." The wording of this canon is identical with c. 968 § 1 of the CIC/1917.

Although this prescription is not indicated as divine law (*ius divinum*), it is nevertheless seen as "definitive doctrine." Canon 750 § 2 CIC states that "definitive doctrines" are to be held under obligation and under threat of a "just penalty" (cf. c. 1371 n. 1), which means that people who do not obey or who reject these "definitive doctrines" are to be punished by severe penalties.

The consequences of these laws and of the underlying doctrines are serious: women are still excluded from the diaconate and "definitively" from priesthood and episcopate. Therefore they are deprived of exercising responsible pastoral ministry (on their own) within priesthood.

As non-ordained persons, women are not capable of exercising the "power of governance" (*potestas iurisdictionis*); as "permanent" lay people they can only "cooperate in the exercise of the same power in accordance with the law"(cf. cc. 129§ 2; 274 § 1). That means, they have no influence (within the parameters of ordained ministry) on the binding doctrine of faith, morals/ethics of the church and on canon law.

The consequences for church practice are the following: despite the worldwide lack of priests, women are not allowed to preside at Eucharistic liturgies; even religious communities, in which very often there are theologically trained women, are dependent on male priests. Women are totally excluded from the official teachings of the church, e.g. at church councils, even if women are personally affected by these teachings. The current Code of Canon Law is compiled exclusively by men. Women belong, per se, to the subordinated lay people who are obliged to obey the "sacred Pastors" (c. 212 § 1). As a consequence of their exclusion from ordination and ordained ministries (c. 1024), the freedom to choose a state of life (c.219) is seriously limited for women in the Roman Catholic Church, although this right, according to the encyclical of Pope John XXIII, *Pacem in terris* (1963), belongs both to the inviolable human rights and to the fundamental rights of all in the church (cf. c. 219).

Historic Background – an Overview

What are the roots of and reasons for this grave oppression and discrimination against women in the Roman Catholic Church?

Of course, churches as well as religious communities are greatly influenced by the surrounding culture and societies. With regard to the status of women this is especially the case. Both the Jewish and the Christian religions developed within a patriarchal environment, so that the traces of it cannot be overlooked in the Holy Scriptures.

In the Hebrew Bible and far beyond one can follow the "tradition" of the discrimination of women, which has left its mark on the relationship between men and women in the church.

Certain biblical texts: the tale of the creation of woman out of Adam, the first trespassing of the divine commandment by Eve and its consequences (Gen 2. 3), above all the misunderstood "threat of punishment" against woman: "You will desire your husband, but he will be your master" (Gen 3:16) – not forgetting the history of the reception and interpretation of these texts from an androcentric perspective – all this together laid the foundation for the biological and moral discrimination against women which runs through the whole history of the church.

Woman is regarded as an inferior, second-rate creature who has no immediate access to God. As such, she is more threatened by evil than is man. Already in the apostolic and post-apostolic literature, the above-mentioned biblical texts are used as arguments against women (cf. 1 Cor 11:3-10; 1 Tim 2:11-14). The last-mentioned text is especially revealing in our context. From the alleged ontological and moral inferiority of women, concrete consequences are drawn concerning their position in the Christian community: "The role of women is to learn, listening quietly and with due submission. I do not permit women to teach or to dictate to men; they should keep quiet. For Adam was created first, and Eve afterwards; moreover it was not Adam who was deceived; it was the woman who, yielding to deception, fell into sin." The subjection of women in marriage and family is also decreed in the so-called "Haustafeln" (cf. Col 3:18; Eph 5:22-33; 1 Pet 3:1-6) and is transferred as a principle of correct behavior into the Christian communities.

Against the predominance of this antifeminist tradition, certain beginnings and examples of a more feminist counter-tradition in the New Testament and in the early church had no chance to push through. As we know, women played an important part in the missionary movement and in the building up of early Christian communities, and they also served as missionary apostles (Junia, Prisca). In the early church, women ministered as deacons, presbyters and even as bishops in certain places, above all in some parts of Southern Italy. (This is well documented, for instance in the research of Ute Eisen and Dorothy Irvin.)

However, as the threefold ministry of diaconate, presbyterate and episcopate became more and more consolidated, women were increasingly driven out of these ministries. Additionally, the purity laws in the Hebrew Bible (cf. Lev 12:1ff; 15:19ff.), which were revived in the Middle Ages, were very disadvantageous for women, so that they were more and more barred from ministries and from the altar.

The extent of discrimination against women is expressed in the denial that woman is created in God's image, (cf. 1 Cor 11:7), an opinion which was passed on through the centuries (cf. Ambroasiaster, 4.c.; Thomas Aquinas, 13.c.).

This long-lasting discrimination against women is finally the basis for their exclusion from ordination, which was decreed in c. 968 § 1 CIC/1917 and is still upheld in the current Code of Canon Law (c.1024).

However, this antifeminist history has been largely ignored by the responsible leaders of the church right up to the present day. This is an intolerable deficit. Instead of taking heed of current scholarly research, which shows that the centuries-old discrimination against women is unjust, present church leaders continue the discrimination against women by whitewashing and covering it up by the constantly repeated axiom: "Women are equal – but other." "Women have a different role compared with men"; therefore ordained ministries allegedly are not necessary for them. The repeated allusion to the "genius of woman" (John Paul II.) serves as appeasement.

The dilemma of the present situation of women in the Roman Catholic Church

If Roman Catholic women try to overcome the burden of their long-lasting devaluation and disadvantage, if they want to get full access to all ordained ministries, they find themselves confronted with almost inaccessible fortress walls.

The following facts, each of them separately and together, are major impediments:

- The Apostolic Letter of John Paul II. *Ordinatio Sacerdotalis* (1994) was pronounced to be "definitive" magisterial doctrine. It can therefore not easily be put aside by subsequent popes. The present pope, Benedict XVI, has made a commitment of continuity with his predecessor. Concerning women's issues in the church, he has not deviated from this promise yet. Therefore, we hardly can expect any reform in this regard during his papacy.

- It is possible that among the bishops there may be some who are open-minded towards women's ordination, at least for women as deacons, but because of their promise of obedience to the pope they will avoid any public deviation in this regard. Most of the bishops, however, cling to the tradition of exclusion of women from ordained ministries. If a future council (when will this happen?) were to debate and decide on women's ordination, we could hardly expect a positive result.

- Reform movements developing from the grassroots, e.g. the We Are Church movement, bounce off the leading authorities of the church on account of its strong hierarchical structure. Until now, these movements could not push through their demands and so they are in danger of tiring.

- Is there any hope for women that this rigid hierarchical system will collapse and the male church will go down in the near future? Church leadership is still working very hard to avoid such a decline by joining together more and more parish communities, at the expense of pastoral ministries and eucharistic liturgies.

**Ordination *contra legem* as a possible way out and
as an impulse for reform.**

Is there any way out of this dilemma? Regarding this hopeless situation, in 2002, seven women started to follow their spiritual calling: they decided to be ordained *contra legem* (c. 1024). This was a public prophetic sign making evident that spiritual callings to ordained ministries cannot be forever suppressed by a law imposed by men on women. These seven women referred to the biblical word: "We must obey God rather than men" (Acts 5:29) and to the many occasions on which Jesus trespassed inhuman laws, declaring: "The Sabbath was made for human beings, not human beings for the Sabbath" (Mk 2:27).

Since this first public ordination ceremony, the movement of womenpriests has been growing fast, above all in the USA. The newly-ordained womenpriests are surrounded by communities who are full of respect for their spiritual calling and charisms. The members of these communities are inspired by the early Christian communities and, like them, they strive to follow the spirit and example of Jesus, in sisterhood and brotherhood, in servant-leadership and compassion.

On this way, a new tradition, contrary to the antifeminist tradition, is being formed within the Roman Catholic Church. If this inclusive, woman-friendly tradition and practice attracts more and more people willing to support the movement, it seems possible that this new tradition, like yeast, will leaven (cf. Mk 13:20.) and thus change the patriarchal structure and behavior of the "official" church. That is our hope!

(**literary reference**: Ida Raming: The Priestly Office of Women: God's Gift to a Renewed Church Second Edition. (A History of Women and Ordination Vol. 2, edited and translated by Bernard Cooke and Gary Macy), The Scarecrow Press, Lanham, Maryland. Toronto. Oxford, 2004)

Ordained a priest: 2002 Passau
Ordained a bishop: 2006 Stuttgart

(Note: Ida Raming was born in 1932 in Fürstenau in northwestern Germany. She studied philosophy, education, theology and German in Münster (Westfalen) and in Freiburg/Breisgau. After her first state examination, in High School Education, she continued theological studies in Münster. Dr. Raming received her doctorate in theology from the University of Münster in 1970. Her thesis, "The Exclusion of Women from Priesthood: Divine Law or Gender Discrimination?" was published in German in 1973 and in English in 1976 and 2004. For several years, Dr. Raming held an academic post in the department of Catholic theology at the University of Münster. Later she was employed as a high school teacher in schools near Münster. From 1984—1993, she served as an advisory member to the feminist theology section of the international theological journal, *Concilium*, while holding several lectureships at theological colleges. Dr. Raming is the author of many books and articles on the history and theology of women, especially on women in the Roman Catholic Church. Finally, she decided that the best – and possibly the only – way forward was to transgress canon 1024 of the Code of Canon Law. On June 29, 2002, Dr. Raming was one of the seven women who were ordained to the Roman Catholic priesthood aboard a ship on the Danube River. She was ordained Bishop Raming in 2006.)

FROM THE INTERNATIONAL DIRECTOR OF FORMATION

Patricia Fresen, Bishop

Patricia Fresen with Olivio Doko, right and Juanita Cordero, front.
Fresen in center

A NEW UNDERSTANDING OF PRIESTLY MINISTRY

Looking at a Church in Crisis
Patricia Fresen

OUR CHURCH IS IN crisis on many fronts. The good news is that responses and solutions to the crisis are emerging and moving us forward in a great paradigm shift. It is a *kairos* time, "when the church is called to return to its authentic, deeper self."[1] There are two particular aspects of the ecclesial crisis on which I wish to focus: liberation from sexism by embodying equality for women and men, especially in ministry; and the shortage of priests in the West, especially in Europe and North America.

Many parishes are being shut down because there are not enough priests. The few priests left have to go around the parishes in turn to celebrate Eucharist and the other sacraments, and in some cases they are able to visit each parish community only once every few months. Priests from the East or Eastern Europe or Africa are imported to minister in Europe and North America, and this often does not work out well. For the "official" church, the need to enforce a rigid model of priesthood, and to insist that it is reserved to celibate males, is more important than the right of communities to celebrate Eucharist.

The sacraments are for the people, and the people are coming up with alternative solutions to the critical shortage of priests, as well as to the unjust exclusion of women from priestly ministry. It is a scandal that "the church that speaks justice to the world, refuses to practice justice within the church itself".[2]

There is now new evidence that women were in ministry in the Church for 1,200 years. The research by Dr. Dorothy Irvin and the

---

[1] Ludwig, Robert A. *Reconstructing Catholicism*. Crossroad (1995) 42.

[2] Ibid, 3.

latest book by Gary Macy are just two examples of the growing body of scholarly literature that give ample evidence of this.

Since the 1960's, the contemporary impetus for women's ordination has been reawakened in Europe and North America. In the 1990's, the group now called Roman Catholic Womenpriests (RCWP) started preparing seriously for ordination and in 2002 they found a bishop who was willing to ordain them. Several of them were subsequently ordained as bishops, so that the ordinations of women could continue. For the sake of credibility and also as a matter of justice, these women are ordained in apostolic succession. Women have the right, not only to be ordained to the diaconate, priesthood and episcopacy, but to be ordained in the same way, in the same tradition, as men. At this early stage of women's ordination, it is important, even essential, to claim this right. The sacrament of Orders is founded on baptism, not on gender.

It is possible that, once women's right to be ordained equally with men, and in the same way, is more firmly established, there may be some new developments. Some of this is already happening, both in RCWP and in the new model of ministry put forward by the Dutch Dominicans. I suggest that our whole understanding of apostolic succession could be considerably broadened. Apostolic succession rightly means that the tradition of laying-on of hands for community ministry comes down to us through the centuries from the time of the early Church, and in fact goes back even beyond that. However, it need not necessarily be limited to the laying-on of hands by the bishop only. When we trace what we call apostolic succession, it usually goes back, in its written form, to some time during the Middle Ages. This is a hierarchical form of apostolic succession, passed down from one bishop to the next. It could still be accepted as apostolic succession, I propose, if the community – not the bishop – were to lay on hands. That would fit the communitarian model.

We also recognize that there are many possible different models of priesthood and of church, and many ways of moving towards justice and equality for women and men. While we move forward along our path, we respect the different paths along which others are walking.

The RCWP Paradigm

Why not build up a "different" model of church and simply "bless" ministries? Since the dualistic system of clerics and laity in the church has become corrupted by the abuse of power, why ordain women to become part of that system?

The questions are good ones. The response is a concise outline of the vision of RC Womenpriests.

We ordain because we are in a transitional time. We need to claim for women their equal right with men to be ordained. And we have no option but to do this *contra legem* (against the law): to break an unjust law and yet to remain firmly within the Roman Catholic Church. This is what we did in South Africa to break down the unjust apartheid system. We had to break the unjust laws, and yet we remained South African. Some South Africans were punished by being imprisoned. The church punished the first seven women ordained in 2002 by excommunicating them. On May 29, 2008, the Congregation for the Doctrine of the Faith issued an "absolute and universal" decree of excommunication that stated:

Regarding the crime of attempting sacred ordination of a woman...Remaining firm on what has been established by canon 1378 of the Canon Law, both he who has attempted to confer holy orders on a woman, and the woman who has attempted to receive the said sacrament, incurs in latae sententiae excommunication, reserved to the Apostolic See.

Please note that excommunication does not put one outside the Church. It is a punishment that forbids one to participate in the sacraments.

People have suggested that we should not ordain women because, by doing so, we are "buying into" the clerical system and becoming part of the clerical caste. But if, in this initial transitional stage, we merely blessed the ministries of everyone, we would do nothing towards claiming equal rights for women in the church and no one would take us seriously as priests. We would be seen as just another sect. We need to take clear action for the equal right of women to be ordained in order to break down the sexism that is so rampant in our hierarchical structures.

In the future, perhaps in the next generation or two, there may well be a return to the practice of the very early Church, when there was no ordination of priests. The people in the community took turns in leading the Eucharist, often depending upon whose home they were meeting in. For now, however, I believe strongly that we need to break the unjust law that excludes women from ordination. We must not try to jump over this stage of claiming justice, but allow the process to evolve organically.

People ask us why we don't simply "leave" our church and be priests in churches where we would be welcomed. We believe we need to reform the church structures from within. Going outside of official church structures, we can achieve nothing. We are already excluded, and leaving would intimate that we accept our exclusion.

By ordaining women, we are re-imagining, restructuring, reshaping the priesthood and therefore the Church:

We believe that it is possible to live and build up a new model of priesthood which, in itself, will help bring about a new model of church. Let me list some of the ways in which we strive to avoid the trap of dualism, clericalism and hierarchy. We do not want to perpetuate the present model of the "providing church" that enables the deplorable passive consumer attitude of its members.

Among the womenpriests, priesthood is not part of a power structure. We see it and try to live it as a ministry of servant-leadership, not as part of a system of domination or exclusion. We avoid using the words "clerics" and "laity." Everyone is included in decision-making. Ordination gives one a different function but not more power. When we in RCWP have a meeting, the bishops and priests do not have more say than anyone else. Leadership is important, but in a model of shared power, a "discipleship of equals."

We recognize the gifts and talents, the responsibility and responsibilities of each person in a differentiation of ministries. We live and work together as a community.

We do not have obligatory celibacy. In fact, we do not link celibacy and priesthood. Our ordained women and men may be married or single, hetero- or homosexual. Some are grandmothers, a few are divorced and/or have had their marriages annulled. We are a cross-section of the Christian community in our lifestyles.

We do not promise obedience to the bishop(s). Among the men, obedience to the bishop is an essential part of the hierarchical structure. We strive to live in prophetic obedience – to find and walk together the "holy road" along which we trust the Spirit is leading us. A symbol of this attitude is that during an ordination the candidates do not kneel or prostrate in front of the bishops, but rather in front of the altar. The bishops and priests sit to the side if it is logistically possible.

In the older worldview, obedience was understood as doing what you were told by those in authority, but obedience is not doing what you are told by anyone else unless you are a child. Obedience – for adults – comes from the Latin ob-audire, attentive listening:

• listening, in the first place, to myself, my own formed conscience, my values, my sense of what is right and wrong; listening to my heart;

• attentive listening to the signs of the times, to what is going on the world and the church, to new levels of awareness and new developments within humanity;

- listening, individually and together, to the Spirit, whom we believe is always moving and awakening us to new levels of awareness. As Isaiah says so often, speaking in God's name: "Listen to me, pay attention and your soul will live" (e.g. 55:3).

Why is this obedience called "prophetic"? I think it is because the prophets, in the Scriptures and in our own times – contemporary prophets like Oscar Romero, Dorothy Day and Nelson Mandela, and yes, the leaders of the women's ordination movement – were and are women and men who "listened to a different drum." They became aware of what was wrong within their own society and they felt impelled to take a stand, to speak out, to name the evil. As we know, those in charge usually do not want to hear what the prophets say, because it means giving up their positions of privilege and power – or at least sharing privilege and power – and once these are shared, the entire system changes from being dualistic to being one in which the equality, dignity and freedom of all are respected.

We are worker-priests. We are financially independent of the Church and we each earn our livelihood in some other way. The financial dependence of priests upon their bishop or their Order is a very strong aspect of the power structure in the hierarchical church.

We eschew titles. We have no equivalent to "Father" once we are ordained. We do not wish to refer to ourselves or anyone else as "Reverend." We do not think we are to be more revered because of ordination.

Vestments and vessels are simple, rather than elaborate or expensive. The bishops do not wear miters, which would make them look taller and more important than everyone else. A bishop's staff is a symbol of being a shepherd, thus pointing to the bishop's pastoral role, but miters, tiaras and elaborate vestments were for kings and emperors, and from the time of Constantine, popes and prelates copied these symbols of temporal power as power became more and more linked to the clerical caste.

We have a communitarian and inclusive model of celebrating Eucharist. The Eucharistic Prayer is often prayed by everyone present, either all together or with different people reading different sections. The words of institution may be said by all present. Communion is distributed by the ministers (bishops, priests, deacons, ministers of the Eucharist) to stress their function of service. The community celebrates the whole Eucharist together, but there is a leader, who may be a man or a woman. We use the words and the rite of Eucharist of the Roman Catholic Church.

We are consciously and deliberately ecumenical. We concelebrate with priests and ministers, women and men, of other traditions, especially with Old Catholics, Lutherans and Episcopalians, and we invite them to our ceremonies and celebrations. We are also open to discussions with them on issues of interest to us all.

We are aware of the danger of buying into, becoming part of, the hierarchical (dualistic) structures, vision and system by becoming members of the clergy. As in the new South Africa, what we have now in a church with ordained women is not perfect. We need to be very careful that we do not, in fact, fall into the trap of taking on the old system, just as in South Africa people need to be very careful that they do not build up another system of racial oppression, this time of Blacks oppressing Whites.

My Journey – and Our Journey

I was born and bred in South Africa. My grandparents had emigrated there, my father's parents from Germany and my mother's from Ireland and England. I grew up in the racially segregated society of South Africa, where people were forcibly separated by law. However, things were changing in South Africa and there was a growing awareness of how wrong apartheid was. It was the Black people themselves who began to take matters into their own hands. We all know that this is usually the way in human society. It is not the oppressors, the ones with all the power and privilege, who come forward to put things right; it is the oppressed, who become aware of their oppression and aware that they need to band together and stand up for their rights, often at great cost. They are the ones who overturn the systems of oppression and bring society one step closer to justice and the recognition of human dignity and human rights.

I never dreamed that my experience of the breaking-down of racism in South Africa would, in part, lead me to where I am today: an ordained Roman Catholic bishop whose journey to ordination has led me to stand up against unjust church laws.

My longing to be a priest began to make itself felt within me during my seven years of studying theology in Rome in the 1980's. Like so many other women, I always suppressed it, since it was unthinkable. But it kept coming back, often at the most unexpected moments.

Back in South Africa, I was invited to join the staff of our national seminary in Pretoria, where I taught systematic theology, homiletics and spirituality for seven years. During those years at the seminary I experienced much gender discrimination, but the desire to minister as a priest was growing stronger. Many people who knew me confirmed their sense of my call to priesthood, including seminarians, priests, friends and even a bishop. No one, however, thought that ordination for women was possible in the Roman Catholic Church.

Then I read about and subsequently met some of the women who had been ordained on the Danube in 2002. They offered to ordain me. It was an offer I could not refuse because I felt so strongly that God was calling me to priesthood and offering me a way.

I was ordained during the Women's Synod in Barcelona in a private ceremony in August, 2003. Because of my ordination, I had to leave the Dominican Order. This was a great sadness for me and my life has changed considerably since then. But, as so many ordained women have discovered, some doors close and others – often ones you never dreamed existed – open for you.

After my ordination, I was asked to coordinate the Program of Preparation for Priesthood for women. I thought that coordinating our program would not be too much work. Seven women had been ordained in 2002. In 2003 there were only a handful of women in the program. But from 2004 onwards, the inquiries and applications started to roll in and since then the numbers have snowballed. There are presently well over 100 women (and a few men) working their way through our program to prepare for priestly ministry, and the total number of ordained women and men, including those ordained in "catacaomb" ordinations, is spiraling upwards toward 100.

One of the most frequently asked questions is: "And what do the ordained women do, once they are ordained, since they will not be accepted into the parishes and dioceses of the R.C. Church?" The answer is that they minister in house churches, reminiscent of the small but growing communities in the early centuries. There are so many people on the fringes of the institutional church, people who are hungry for a community in which they can feel at home. It is mostly these people who form communities around our ordained womenpriests. The house churches start small, but many have grown to the point that it is no longer possible to meet in people's homes and they find a chapel or a church building which they rent, or which is freely offered to them, where the community can gather. What is at work here is the *sensus fidelium*, the inner sense of the faithful, that this is the right way to go and that the Spirit is leading them in this direction. The people are ready. The time is now.

Could we be in the midst of an evolutionary leap in the life of the Church – a leap which is part of the reconstruction of the Church, the

Church of tomorrow, the Church that we believe is closer to the community Jesus had in mind?

Ordained a priest: 2003, Barcelona, Spain
Ordained a bishop: 2005, Austria

(Note: Patricia Fresen was born and raised in South Africa. She joined the Dominicans after leaving school. Her first degrees were in Arts and Education. She taught in convent high schools for many years, and was also in school administration. Then she studied theology for seven years in Rome, at the University of St. Thomas and the Gregoriana, and obtained a Licentiate in Theology. Returning to South Africa in 1988, she was invited to join the faculty of the National Seminary of Pretoria, where she taught sacramental theology, spirituality and homiletics. Meanwhile, she completed her doctoral studies and thesis, and earned the Doctorate of Theology in May, 1996, through the University of South Africa. From 1999—2003, Dr. Fresen was on the faculty of the Catholic University in Johannesburg. In August, 2003, she was ordained a priest. As a result, Dr. Fresen had to leave the Dominicans, and she moved to Germany She is currently Coordinator of the Training Program in Preparation for the Priesthood for Roman Catholic Womenpriests. In 2005, she was ordained a bishop to ensure that the ordination of women will continue. Bishop Fresen has presided at ordinations in Europe, Canada and the USA.)

FROM THE FIRST NORTH AMERICAN BISHOP

Dana Reynolds, Bishop

Bishops Gisela Forster and Dana Reynolds, priest Suzanne Thiel,
Bishops Ida Raming and Patricia Fresen.

THE MYSTICAL HEART OF TABLE COMMUNITY

Dana Reynolds

"Y OU SAY GOD SPEAKS to you – but it's only your imagination."
These words were declared to Joan of Arc by the tribunal of
inquisitors at her trial for heresy in the spring of 1431. She replied
calmly, "...and how else would God speak to me but through my
imagination?"

This is the statement of a French peasant girl who became the
most notable warrior saint of the Christian calendar. She followed
Divine direction given to her through Saint Margaret, Saint Michael,
and Saint Catherine. These "voices" guided her to leave home and
family, and dress in men's clothing, to lead an army and help crown a
king. She often saw the saints that spoke to her and it is said that white
butterflies followed her whenever she rode into battle. The fact that she
would not deny her mystical guidance ultimately led to her death at a
fiery stake. She was nineteen.

Saint Joan's simple response to the churchmen who would
ultimately decide her fate, resonates within my spirit. It has provided
me with inspiration for my calling as a woman priest, a spiritual
director, a mentor for women, and most recently as one preparing for
ordination to the episcopacy.

In hindsight, I realize that my early background as a visual artist
was a pathway to the deepening of my relationship with God.
Whenever I was sketching ideas, writing an icon, or creating a visual
journal, I felt connected creatively to a place I eventually named the
sacred imagination. This metaphoric field of pure potential within each
of us is the place where the Holy Spirit fuels creativity, sparks dreams
and visions, and seeds our callings.

The sacred imagination is the inner space where God speaks to us,
sometimes clearly and directly and sometimes in a whisper. Saint Joan
knew this territory well, and inspired by the mystics of the early Church

and the Middle Ages, I have been experiencing an ongoing exploration of the mystery of God's symbolic language.

Three hundred years before Saint Joan's voices, Hildegard of Bingen, a Benedictine abbess in Rhineland, began dictating her "visions" to a young monk. Some time later these recordings evolved into her book, *Scivias* ("Know the Ways"), containing illuminations depicting Hildegard's visionary revelations. These exquisitely rendered medieval illustrations are rich with symbolic imagery and meaning. Unlike Saint Joan, Hildegard (and her visions), after being investigated by a commission of churchmen, was given papal approval. She received the Church's permission to continue her creative work, and she did so with fervor.

She was a scientist, poet, painter, healer, musician, playwright, prophet, preacher, and social critic. To read her *Book of Divine Works* is to encounter a reuniting of science, religion, and creativity. In 1979, Pope John Paul II, in celebration of the 800th anniversary of Hildegard's death, referred to her as "an outstanding saint...a light to her people and her time (who) shines out more brightly today."

Saint Hildegard and Saint Joan are but two examples of many individuals throughout history who came to be known as mystics, those who encountered the Divine through visions, voices, and other ecstatic experiences. Mysticism is defined by Webster's Collegiate Dictionary as "the experience of mystical union or direct communion with ultimate reality reported by mystics." A definition of mystical is "having spiritual meaning or reality that is neither apparent to the senses nor obvious to the intelligence."

Taking one more step, consider the word "mystery." According to Webster, the first definition is "a religious truth that one can know only by revelation and cannot fully understand." Mystery seems to be an accompaniment to mysticism. Revelation seems to be the common denominator of reported mystical experiences.

In studies to examine the phenomena of cosmic illuminations (visions of ineffable Light) among diverse groups, including an Eskimo shaman, Saint Paul, and an American businessman, Mircea Eliade came to some general conclusions.

It is important to stress that whatever the nature and intensity of an experience of the Light, it always evolves into religious experience. ...(these encounters) bring a man/a woman out of the worldly Universe or historical situation, and project him/her into a Universe different in quality, an entirely different world, transcendent and holy...in brief, existence as a divine creation, or the world sanctified by the presence of God.

Entering a state of "existence as a divine creation," feeling oneself in the literal presence of God, connects one to the mystery. In this mystical place, the gateway between heaven and earth, revelations are gifted, sometimes through the voices of angels, sometimes through symbolic visions.

Often, the moment of being projected into a "Universe different in quality" is not as dramatic as the recorded experiences of the saints, yet equally profound. Perhaps the inexplicable occurs during an early morning walk. A deer emerges from the fog, antlers glistening, stately and silent. Eye to eye, the gaze penetrates the human's soul. For an instant there is super-eminent connection, and the accompanying cellular realization that both stag and mortal are from the hands of the same Creator. There is no separation. There is a feeling of oneness with all creation. This singular transcendent moment inspires a desire to become an advocate for animal rights. In time, the revelation born from this mystical experience is put into action. Animal life is protected. A human life is enriched. The covenant that commenced on a foggy morning walk has been sealed.

Mysticism is returning to our culture. Books on the subject of life-changing moments of divinely inspired insights, experiences of Light, and miracles, fill the shelves of bookstores. The ancient spiritual mystical traditions of walking the labyrinth and saying the rosary are reemerging. Encounters with angels and the Blessed Virgin abound.

While ministering to women for the past twenty years, through spiritual direction and spiritual/creative retreats and workshops, I have heard countless stories of women's dreams and visions – dreams and visions that have altered the course of women's lives, deepened their faith, and called them into a personal working relationship with the Divine.

My understanding of the sacred imagination, and the subsequent focus of my ministry centering on the Mystical Heart and Visual Prayer, has gradually emerged from a four-part experience, including: my dream life and reflections; an independent study of the early women Christian mystics and the Beguines; exploration of sacred art-making and journaling; and the inspiration of the scriptural story from Luke about Jesus' visit with Martha and Mary in Bethany. These experiences have led me on an inner pilgrimage, a co-creative journey with Spirit, infused with sacred mystery, celebratory liturgies, and visual prayer as a means of expressing my ministry in tangible ways. I will share here the basic concepts of my understanding of the Mystical Heart and its relationship to table community.

The Mystical Heart: A Cartography of the Soul

Imagine the heart, the Sacred Heart of Christ, as the heart of universal peace, wisdom, and compassion. Now imagine that the unending heartbeat, the rhythm of Jesus' Sacred Heart, is in fact unified with the tempo of creation itself. Within this universal pulse exists a vast library, containing alchemical prescriptions for the infusion of harmony and healing for the human condition. Through prayerful intercession, purification of the senses, renewal of the spirit, and sacred creative practices, alignment of one's heartbeat with the heartbeat of Christ transforms the soul into a conduit for grace.

The human heart is the womb of Divine love. In the Mystical Heart there are four chambers. (Visualize this as a template or overlay that rests atop the anatomical heart.) Each chamber is a vessel for a particular grace associated with love, including compassion, acceptance, forgiveness, and faith.

The heart must be broken open to deliver God's love through the four graces. The breaking open of the heart is accomplished through the activation and purification of the senses. Our senses – touch, taste, smell, sight, hearing, and intuiting – are our message receptors for mystical and sacred understanding.

Christ's Sacred Heart exudes radical love, love that is rooted in the foundation of creation. God's creative love that birthed the universe is the Sacred Heart. We come from the source of that Divine love. Our spirits long to reconnect to the fire, the creative and generative momentum that await our remembering through the acknowledgement and activation of the senses. When the senses are revered as the message-carriers for God, quickening of the heart occurs and we become conduits for God's grace to flow to us and through us.

Effort + Intention/Awareness = Movement of Grace

Spiritual labor is the process to birthing the love of God/God's love into life. The paradox is that we are always in union with God, but often in our busyness we are unaware of the Divine presence within. Finding the places in one's life that create openings to hearing the Mystical Heartbeat of creation will, over time, begin to engage the senses, activate the dreams of sleep and the visions of day, and inspire awareness of the territory of the sacred imagination.

The story of Mary and Martha (Luke 10:38-41) teaches us the importance of contemplation and table community as foundational nourishment for our mystical hearts.

As they traveled, Jesus entered a village where a woman named Martha welcomed him to her home. She had a sister named Mary, who seated herself at Jesus' feet and listened to his words. Martha who was busy with all the details of hospitality, came to Jesus and said, "Rabbi, don't you care that my sister has left me all alone to do the household tasks? Tell her to help me!"

Jesus replied, "Martha, Martha! You're anxious and upset about so many things, but only a few things are necessary – really only one. Mary has chosen the better part, and she won't be deprived of it."

Contemplation and Table Community

As I prepared for ordination to the episcopacy, I was acutely aware that as Roman Catholic women priests, deacons, and bishops we are a discipleship of equals who are reclaiming the table ministry of Eucharistic celebration and our apostolic authority as servant leaders. This *anamnesis,* whereby the past is made present again in this time and this place, is a revivification of the early Church when women were priests, deacons, and bishops in full apostolic authority.

In my pastoral ministry contemplation, the Mary story is essential to the nourishment and well-being of my mystical heart and the mystical hearts of the women I have been called to serve. Likewise, table community, celebration of the Eucharist and the celebration of liturgy (the Martha story) are born from the space of contemplation into sacred form and holy active sharing.

Our liturgies, the table communities we co-create with the Holy Spirit and one another, become our visual prayers. Enlivening the symbols of our faith – the bread (the Body of Christ), the wine (the Blood of Christ), and the table (the place where we meet to share the Sacrament, the holy meal) – with renewed vitality and inclusivity, we are drawing from the spirits of Mary and Martha as we re-imagine a Church where all are welcome: a Church of Divine Wonder where we partake of the Bread of Life as a table community where no one is turned away; and a place where the living waters flow forth with spirit, where the wisdom of the ancients and the Word of God are celebrated with prayer, song, and shared story.

Our table communities exemplify the Mystical Heart with its chambers of compassion, acceptance, forgiveness, and faith. Spending time in contemplation of these four graces fortifies the spirit, and fosters a place within for inspiration for liturgy and agape readiness.

My ministry calls me to nourish the creative spirits, the sacred imaginations, of those I minister to. The sacred arts, including spiritual journaling, writing/reading ecstatic poetry, praying with icons, meditating with sacred music, creating visual prayers (altars, intentional collage), and liturgical dance, are tools to enrich

41

contemplation and daily spiritual practice. Engaging in these contemplative exercises enriches the soil of the sacred imagination and fertilizes the seeds of calling that God instills.

Sharing in table community, celebrating Eucharistic liturgies, and welcoming all to the table engages our Martha and Mary spirits of servant leadership and full apostolic authority. Transformation and activation of the mystical human heart are the result when those who come to the table experience a renaissance of spirit through remembering that they are the People of God. All present begin to realize, *"We are Church!"*

When I think of my *contra legem* act of becoming a woman priest, I remember Joan of Arc, who was *contra legem* for her time. I am called to join my pilgrim sisters and brothers on the Holy Road, as together we are re-imagining the Roman Catholic Church.

This is a time of renaissance, of new birth as a discipleship of equals in table community. A renaissance calls upon our creativity and requires quickening of the human mystical heart. God is calling us forth. It's a time of listening, and of sacred co-creation with the Divine. As Saint Joan reminds us: *How else would God speak to us, but through our imaginations?*

Ordained a priest: 2006, Pittsburgh
Ordained a bishop: 2008, Stuttgart

FROM OUR MEDIA REPRESENTATIVE

Bridget Mary Meehan, Priest

Bridget Mary Meehan with Mary, Mother of Jesus House Church,
Sarasota, Florida

HOUSE CHURCHES

Back to Basics: Christ-Centered, Spirit-Empowered Communities
Bridget Mary Meehan

S OME LIKE IT BECAUSE everybody can share their thoughts about Gospel-living at the homily. Some like it because the congregation knows one another and are like extended family. Some like it because they know the people with whom they worship. Some like it because the priest is a woman. We are getting back to basics, to the early church model of Christ-centered, Spirit-empowered gatherings in which people from all walks of life come together to worship and share their lives as pilgrims on a sacred journey, and to celebrate the Eucharist.

Since I am Irish by birth, offering hospitality is part of my cultural inheritance. My 83 year-old dad and I always have a kettle on the boil. We love to invite people to sing and dance in our home. Our family in Ireland was known as the "musical Meehan's" because several of Dad's brothers played musical instruments in the Ballyroan Brass Band. Our motto is *caed mile a failte*, a hundred thousand welcomes to all who come into our home. We are people-friendly. Our liturgies are festive, full of song, music, clapping, singing, and even swaying now and again! One woman, Marie, who had been divorced and remarried, cried when she received communion at our house church last spring. After a hostile encounter with a priest years ago, she felt unworthy to receive the Eucharist in her parish community. She says, "I feel like I have come home at last." Marie has invited me to celebrate Mass in her home, with her family and friends, for an upcoming anniversary celebration.

The Roman Catholic Womenpriests communities are finding that the house church setting is full of possibilities for a renewed grassroots church to flourish. We are called forth from the local community to serve the local community. Now a distinguished religious order is affirming that a faith community can select its own leadership and celebrate Eucharist, just like the early churches did (see below).

44

So it appears that the Church has come full circle and we are back to basics. Scholars mention five different house churches in the New Testament. Prisca had a church in her home. "My greetings to Prisca and Aquila (her husband) my co-workers in Christ Jesus who risked their necks to save my life....My greetings also to the church that meets at their house." The church gathered in their home in Rome, (Rom16:3-5), and in Corinth and Ephesus (Acts 18:18; 2 Tim 4:19; 1 Cor 16:19). Lydia, the first Christian convert in Europe, began a church in Philippi. A group of Christians gathered in her home. The "house church" became a popular meeting place for eucharistic liturgies and provided safe haven for persecuted Christians. After Paul's release from prison, for freeing a female slave from demonic possession, Paul and Silas went immediately to Lydia's house and "encouraged the brothers and sisters there" (Acts 16:40). Mary, mother of John Mark, who was an independent woman with a spacious home, was a leader of one of the house churches in Jerusalem Some scholars believe that Greek Christians met in her home and that she presided at Eucharist there, and that her home was the headquarters of the Jerusalem Church (see Bridget Mary Meehan, *Praying with Women of the Bible*, pp. 120-135).

Therefore, it is evident that in the early Church, the Christian communities met for worship and prayer in homes and that, most likely, women presided at the Eucharist. Although the Christian Scripture does not reveal who among the early Christians presided over these sacred meals, one can assume that it was the household leader. In that society, women were the leaders in the home, men in the marketplace. Hence, it is probable that these women functioned in the role that later would be identified as presbyter, or priest. As household heads these women sang songs of praise, broke the bread, blessed the cup, and shared it with their guests in a communal meal.

Contemporary theologians remind us that the gathered assembly, the entire community is the celebrant of Eucharist. It is the community that "does" the Eucharist, not the presider alone (see Bernard Cooke, *The Future of Eucharist*, p. 32). Therefore, it is appropriate that the community, not the priest alone, says the words of consecration together. Gary Macy, chairperson of the Theology and Religious Studies Department at the University of San Diego, concludes that, in the understanding of the medieval mind, regardless of who spoke the words of consecration – man or woman, presider or community – the Christ-presence became a reality in the midst of the assembly. In "Church and Ministry," their newly released document, the Dominicans put forward the following "new possibilities."

45

"Men and women can be chosen to preside at the Eucharist by the church community; that is, 'from below,' and can then ask a local bishop to ordain these people 'from above.'" "If, however, 'a bishop should refuse a confirmation or ordination' of such an individual 'on the basis of arguments not involving the essence of the Eucharist," such as a requirement that deacons or priests be celibate, parishes may move forward without the bishop's participation, remaining confident "that they are able to celebrate a real and genuine Eucharist when they are together in prayer and share bread and wine.'" In fact, Dominican theologian, Fr. Edward Schillebeeckx in his book, *Ministry: Leadership in the Community of Jesus Christ*, pointed out "that the Council of Chalcedon, in the fifth century, had declared any ordination of a priest or deacon illegal, as well as null and void, unless the person being ordained had been chosen by a particular community to be its leader" (*National Catholic Reporter*, December 14, 2007).

At the dawning of the 21st century, Catholic worship, centered in the eucharistic thanksgiving and self-giving of Jesus, is once again being celebrated in house churches. Roman Catholic Womenpriests are leading the way in reclaiming the ancient tradition of eucharistic table sharing that builds community. Like the holy women and men of the early Church, we are gathering together to break open our lives, to share bread and wine in memory of Jesus, and to live the Christ-presence in our work for justice, peace and equality in our world. In Roman Catholic Womenpriest communities, it is the community that prays the consecratory words in the celebration of Eucharist. We have embraced the early churches' practice that the Eucharist belongs to the community and a genuine Eucharist happens when a community gathers to share the sacred bread and wine. Dr. Judith Lee, who came to one of our liturgies in Sarasota, summed up the vision of contemporary house churches in the ministry of the Catholic faithful: "It is a community of equals before God, empowered to go out and be the arms and hands of Christ in the world. Let the people say Amen! They already have!"

Ordained a priest: 2006, Pittsburgh

Marie Bouclin, Priest

Ordination Liturgy in Toronto in 2007. From left to right are Mary Ellen Robertson, Cheryl Bristol, Marie Bouclin, Joan Houk, Patricia Fresen, Michele Birch-Conery, Dagmar Braun Celeste, Jim Lauder, Monica Kilburn-Smith and Alice Iaquinta.

CALL TO MINISTRY

Binding the Wounds of Clergy Abuse
Marie Bouclin

W HO WILL MINISTER TO the women?" Twice I put that question to my diocesan bishop. The first time, it was in response to a perceived need for spiritual support and renewal among lay pastoral assistants. The diocesan priests and deacons had time off for an annual retreat, and funds were made available for days of recollection and attending conferences to further their spiritual growth. The lay pastoral assistants, mostly women, were left to their own resources. They had to study and attend a retreat during their holiday time and at their own expense, unless they were members of a religious order. There was no answer to my query.

The second time I asked about ministering to women was when I expressed concern about healing the spiritual wounds of women who were victims of clergy sexual abuse. The answer I received to this question was, "Marie, all those women want is money." To which I countered, "No, Bishop, they want healing."

I had experienced first hand the sting of clergy abuse of power. My suitability for church employment was questioned after five years of service as executive secretary to a bishop. A reporter had quoted me in the local press as saying that the Roman Catholic Church discriminates against women in its employment practices. The bishop gave me the choice of resigning or accepting to work in a back office where I would have no contact with the public. After a month "in the back office" and much prayer, I felt I had no choice but to leave. In the months that followed, many women called to ensure me of their friendship and support – and to recount their personal stories of unexplained dismissal from church work.

Along with the stories of abuse of power by clergy in the workplace came even more disturbing stories of sexual abuse. The pattern was disturbingly similar: the pastor or spiritual director persuaded a vulnerable woman to engage in a sexual relationship with him – purportedly for the good of her soul. The most troubling part of all was that the leadership of the Roman Catholic Church seemed to have no inkling of the seriousness of the damage done. Betrayed and heartbroken, often physically ill, these women had lost all faith in the Church and the God it claimed to serve. Yet there was no perceived need to care for the wounds of what can only be called rape of the soul. Victims were told to forgive and move on, and it was often hinted that the women themselves were responsible for whatever pain they had suffered.

As more and more cases of sexual abuse were uncovered, dioceses began establishing protocols for dealing with the problem, usually by providing funds so women could access counselling and mental health care. The question still remained as to who would bind the spiritual wounds and help survivors recover their lost faith. Most abused women wanted no part of a religion whose only ministers were men.

At the root of my call to ministry was the desire to reach out to women who had been assaulted, harassed, and exploited by clergy. I prayed to be an instrument by which they could rekindle their faith in the Divine as loving friend and compassionate Healer. The struggle for justice within the Church led me to seek like-minded Catholics in a variety of reform groups. I renewed my membership in the Catholic Network for Women's Equality (CNWE), whose mission is to "enable women to name their giftedness and from that awareness to effect structural change in the church...." Through CNWE, I became involved in the women's ordination movement both nationally and internationally. In the meantime, I also returned to the study of theology, which became a passion. I had reached an age where a teaching career was unlikely to open up for me, so I continued working as a freelance translator specialized in the area of religion and ethics.

In 1996, I was approached by a friend to start a support group for abused women. I declined at first, using the pretext that I needed to finish my Masters degree in theology. Truth be told, I did not feel I had the required pastoral training to help these women. So, instead of volunteering to counsel victims and survivors, I chose to document cases of clergy abuse of power. I focused on the damage suffered by victims, and then established some relationship between the Church's exclusion of women from Holy Orders (and full equality within the Body of Christ) and the impunity with which men could abuse their priestly power. My hope was to propose to survivors a path to spiritual recovery, to regain some sense of spiritual well-being through a new relationship with the Divine. The publication of my thesis led to my being invited to offer workshops for women victims and write articles on the subject of clergy abuse of power. I could use my voice to tell the abused women's stories so that others might recognize themselves and seek help. But I did not feel qualified to minister in any real way to the victims themselves.

Some of them still held a glimmer of belief in the power of the sacraments to be a source of grace and healing in their lives. But the sacraments could only be received at the hands of men. Women survivors of abuse and the Holy Spirit both seemed to be calling me to become a sacramental minister.

In 2000, I had the opportunity to train under Reverend Dr. Marie Fortune of the FaithTrust Institute. According to Marie Fortune, it was not until women were ordained in the Protestant churches that stories of sexual abuse by clergy began to be believed. I was one of twelve women attending her course, the only one belonging to a denomination that did not ordain women. I decided that day to channel my anger and frustration into more energetic dedication to the goals of CNWE and Women's Ordination Worldwide (WOW). In 2002, as CNWE's delegate to the WOW Steering Committee meeting in Salzbourg, Austria, I was invited to the first *contra legem* ordinations on the Danube. That invitation filled me with hope. Finally, I thought, there are members of the hierarchy who are prepared to break ranks and move forward on the women's ordination issue!

It was through the WOW Steering Committee that I met Dr. Patricia Fresen in 2004. Patricia's reputation as a feminist theologian was well-known internationally, and she had been ordained by two members of the Danube Seven, now bishops Dr. Gisela Forster and Christine Mayr Lumetzberger. I told Patricia why I was committed to the work of WOW, and about the need I saw to reach out to Catholic women who had left the Church because a priest had abused them. She felt that perhaps the Spirit was calling me to minister to these women – as a priest. We agreed that as soon as my mandate as WOW coordinator ended, I would apply to the RCWP preparation program.

And so, in August 2006, I was ordained a deacon by Bishop Patricia Fresen in an intimate ceremony at a friend's cottage, attended only by family, close friends and the members of my small faith community. Bishop Patricia, my spiritual director, and the members of my small faith community envisioned my priestly ministry as working with the wounded and alienated women of the Roman Catholic Church. On May 25, 2007 Bishop Patricia ordained me to the priesthood in Toronto, Ontario.

I understand my ministry as a personal response to two passages from the Gospel of Luke. In the King James version, Jesus proclaims that the Spirit has anointed him "to heal the broken-hearted" (4:18). The adult women who shared with me their stories of sexual abuse at the hands of a priest were indeed broken-hearted. The courts who deal with these cases and the counselors who try to help these women recover from the abuse may well judge the behavior of the priest as an abuse of power, professional misconduct and a breach of fiduciary trust. And rightly so. But for those of us who are given a glimpse into the hearts and souls of these women, we discover that these women have been sexually seduced, emotionally violated, and had their consciences raped. Men who claim to represent God have told them that having sexual relations with a priest – a man who has made a vow of celibacy – is not immoral but a misguided understanding of chastity. Men who are ministers of the sacraments of the Church have told women that satisfying the sexual needs of a priest is offering a sacrifice pleasing to God. Vulnerable women, women whose marriage has failed, women who were still grieving the death of a husband, vowed religious struggling with their sexual orientation in a church that still teaches that homosexuality is fundamentally disordered, women whose relationships with men have involved a violent father, brother or husband – these are the women who were seduced by a priest who is also a sexual predator. All of these women heard from the mouth of their abuser, "I love you. I know what you need and I can give you the love you need." And for a while, these women believed those words, until the relationship came to an end – when the priest had no use for them, when they discovered they were one of many women filling a need in the priest's life, or when the priest was publicly denounced or reported to the police or his bishop.

These women were taught to believe that priests do not lie. Priests are invested with Holy Orders; they are therefore holy men. These women were taught that priests speak for God and act in God's name, and that only priests – always male – have been entrusted with the most sacred source of grace, the Eucharist. These women were taught that faith in God means unquestioning intellectual assent to unchallengeable beliefs, and that salvation hinges on obeying the teachings of the Church as transmitted by the priest. It is therefore not surprising that when these women realize they have been seduced, violated and betrayed, they lose all faith in the ministers of the Church and the God they claim to represent.

Ministering to these women is a huge challenge. So many questions were surfacing in my mind. How can I possibly convince these women that they can enter into relationship with a Divine Reality that loves them and wants them healthy and happy? How do I help to

51

heal the broken hearts of women who were abused as children or as vulnerable adults? Can I possibly model a different kind of priestly, Christ-like presence? Can I really be an instrument of God, to rekindle faith in women who are so wounded that they are spiritually crippled? Will God use me to touch their hearts and souls so these women can once again "stand up straight and praise God" (Luke 13:11-13)?

The wounded women of the Roman Catholic Church need ministers who will come to them *in persona Christi*, with the love and compassion of Christ. They cannot wait for the institution to reform, for the Vatican bureaucracy to change canon 1024 – which only allows men to become ministers of the channels of grace we call the sacraments. They cannot wait for Rome to give its permission for women to preach the Living Word. They cannot wait for Rome to give its permission for women to gather people to remember Jesus in the breaking of the Bread and the raising of the Cup of thanksgiving. Women who have suffered violence at the hands of a priest know full well that as long as there are no women standing "in loco Christi" at the altar, all women are at risk of being raped and exploited and harassed with impunity. They know in their flesh and bones that in the current patriarchal mindset women are expendable, still "less than" men, in spite of all claims in Scripture – and even in Magisterial teaching – that women and men are created equal. It was this realization, so succinctly put by Sister Myra Poole at the 2005 WOW Conference, which convinced me that being ordained *contra legem* was obeying God and not man. Following the Spirit who was calling women to priesthood was more important than cowing to the dictates of Canon Law. The fear of excommunication gradually lost all its power over me. I took comfort in the words of Paul, who proclaimed that "nothing" – not an outdated, monarchical, legalistic, power-driven, oppressive church system; no priest, no bishop, not even a pope – "can separate us from the love of God in Christ Jesus" (Romans 8:39). Being excluded from communion in a Roman Catholic church because of an unjust and oppressive law could not cut me off from the love of Christ.

"We are not ordained for ourselves." These words were spoken to Patricia Fresen when she was asked to become a bishop, and these words would become a mantra for Roman Catholic Womenpriests. The day after my ordination, Gary O'Dwyer of Cobourg, Ontario invited me to provide sacramental services to his faith community. Christ the Servant Church, which met for Sunday worship at the Community Centre in Cold Springs, Ontario, began as an offshoot of St. Michael's parish in Cobourg. Their pastor, Fr. Ed Cachia, had been dismissed and subsequently excommunicated because he would not retract his statement, made at the time of the RCWP ordinations on the St. Lawrence in 2005, that it was time for the Vatican to open the discussion on women's ordination. A community of supporters gathered around him, forming a new community called Christ the Servant. After a few months, however, Fr. Ed could seemingly not cope with the isolation of being ostracized by his fellow priests, and he abandoned the community. Nonetheless, Christ the Servant community gathered between fifty and one hundred people from a radius of about sixty miles for a communion service each Sunday. They set up a Church Board for governance, outreach programs for visiting the sick and elderly, Bible and book studies, and they sponsor a missionary Sister. Their mission statement proposes a model of renewed Catholic Church based on the teachings of the Second Vatican Council. I was truly honored to be invited to preside at Eucharist for the first time on June 12, 2007, the Feast of Corpus Christi, and to preach on the Eucharist as "the source and summit of the life of the Church."[3] Because I live some three hundred miles from Cobourg, I accepted to become their associate, part-time pastor. Recently, Christ the Servant community and I have entered into a covenant partnership with Bishop Kevin Fitzgerald of the Community Catholic Church (formerly Old Catholic Church), who has become their full-time pastor.

Parish ministry was not what I foresaw as my ministry, though I did see myself responding to calls to celebrate the sacraments, especially Eucharist, with small groups of women in their homes. Several invitations have been extended to me to celebrate home Eucharists with distanced or disenfranchised Catholics. The numbers of house churches are growing, and these communities are supporting my ministry financially so that I can continue to make myself available for retreats and workshops for adult survivors of clergy sexual abuse.

Dr. Georgia E. Fuller wrote that we must be "open to God's surprises, God's merciful healing for us, and God's leading for us to be healers for other members of God's good creation."[4] We may not know where our priestly ordination will take us in the service of God's people. Because we are a new community, there are pressing needs to be met: establishing structures for a new initiative within the church, recruiting and mentoring new candidates to the priesthood, and interacting with the media. Many of us in RCWP have had to wear

---

[3] *Lumen Gentium*, # 11, The Documents of Vatican II.

[4] Fuller, Dr. Georgia E., MTS, Ph.D. *Discerning God's Spirit in the Quaker Tradition*. Virginia Theological Seminary, July 2006.

many hats, much to our surprise. But I must say that among God's surprises, I have found the most delightful is the joy of proclaiming God's abundant love through the breaking open of the Word and the Bread with women in search of spiritual healing.

Ordained a priest: 2007, Ontario

Eileen McCafferty DiFranco, Priest
Andrea Johnson, Priest
Gabriella Verlardi Ward, Priest

Ordination Liturgy in New York 2007. Eileen Di Franco is standing and seated (from left to right), are Andrea Johnson, Eleonora Marinaro, Gloria Ray Carpeneto and Gabriella Velardi Ward.

Andrea Johnson presides at Mass on occasion of Pope Benedict's visit to Washington DC. Standing to her left is priest Rose Marie Hudson.

A *CONTRA LEGEM* LIFE

Eileen McCafferty DiFranco

ROBERT FROST WROTE THAT two roads diverged in a yellow wood. For women throughout the millennia, there were only these two roads. Deeply creased by ruts made by generations of women on forced marches, one road led to marriage and motherhood, the other to the convent. While a faint trail called "spinsterhood" joined the others in a most oblique fashion, it was overgrown and covered with vines destined to trip up all but the most hardy. The "wise" avoided it at all costs. To be unencumbered by man, either husband or Father God, was simply not to be.

Faint glimmerings of these two roads appeared in early childhood when my parents bought me dolls and my maternal grandmother nudged me towards the convent. I chaffed at these limitations. Why couldn't I be whatever I wanted to be? There had to be other roads. Who wanted to cook and clean when one could be a frontiersman and wear a coonskin cap like my hero, Davy Crockett? Why did I need to wear a dress and be a "lady" when all I wanted to do was run around and play with the boys? Why was it a problem to have the dirtiest female face on the block while shooting marbles in the middle of Livingston Street with boys who were far dirtier than I?

My *contra legem* behavior began when I walked into kindergarten, the only girl with a Davy Crockett school bag. At seven, I beat up Johnny Lees because he dared to suggest that Jesus was a boy. At ten, I was infuriated when I learned that only males could be altar boys, especially since I was smarter than the lot of them. Who made up this stuff?

As with any "revolution," the seeds for my *contra legem* behavior were planted long before their expression by conversations around the family kitchen table and at family gatherings. Observant Catholics to a man and woman, the adults in my family were keen observers of human behavior with a fine-tuned sense of hypocrisy that wore off on us kids. My paternal Aunt Nellie lived to be one hundred. The oldest of eight and well acquainted with the drudgeries of parenthood, Aunt Nellie often compared life in the rectory with the young women made old and poor by too frequent childbearing. She often told me of couples who buried child after child, unknowing victims of the recently discovered RH factor, and of families terrorized by drunken fathers whose mothers were counseled in confession to "offer it up."

My maternal Aunt Peg ate dinner with us every night. Aunt Peg was one of those women who unwilling walked the trail of spinsterhood for most of her life. As secretary for a large company, Aunt Peg became friends with many of her office mates who were not necessarily Catholic, and got to know them as people rather than religious aliens or near occasions of sin. One friend asked her to be her maid of honor and Aunt Peg agreed. After the wedding Aunt Peg felt compelled to go to confession and ask forgiveness for her participation in a Protestant service. The priest told her that he didn't know if he could forgive such an egregious sin. The four of us kids sat wide-eyed as she told us a story that might well separate us from our beloved aunt for all eternity. Aunt Peg looked around at us, put her fork down and asked, "Do you know what I think?" We waited expectantly for her answer. "I think," she said, "that the priest is full of shit." We let our breath out in collective relief, our heavenly family unity assured.

Like Aunt Peg and Aunt Nellie, I fully expected the things I saw to make sense. When they didn't, I needed answers. Grammar rules that declared the use of masculine pronouns with the dictum "masculine by preference." Why? Who said so? Why not the opposite? Tradition and authority made no sense to me if it didn't make sense in my life experience. Why the insistence on male altar servers, many who by seventh grade were drinking on the railroad tracks or smoking in the alleyways? Just what benefit did these male "dangly parts" enjoy in isolation from virtue and character? Was there something about boys that made them better than girls? If there was, I couldn't find it. No man I knew looked or acted like Jesus.

Not having those body parts led to a bad case of early onset cognitive dissonance. I often watched the women on their knees in dresses scrubbing the altar steps, their heads covered by lace mantillas, while "Father" walked out of the church door, lit up his cigar, and made his way to his sleek black car. I watched the sisters in their uncomfortable habits, starched linens forever creasing their foreheads, their shaved heads covered with high headdresses, walk to communion with their faces covered by their veils. What was so wrong with their bodies that they needed to cover them up? Why was the answer always, "just because," or, "God said so"?

My maternal grandmother had often told me that I should be a nun because nuns had "no worries." They had a permanent roof over their heads and three square meals a day. Just the thought of being dressed in hot, oppressive, uncomfortable clothes – including, I imagined, a hated garter belt and stockings – for the remainder of my natural life made me exclaim in alarm, "No, Nana, I don't think the convent is for me." Surely a girl could love and serve God without having to shave her head or wear a garter belt for the rest of her life.

I began reading Freud when I was sixteen. During a study period, I was assigned to be a hall monitor outside of the main office. Sister Mary Leona saw my nose buried in a book and asked what I was reading. When I showed her the book by Freud, she clucked her tongue and warned, "I wouldn't read him if I were you. He will give the wrong ideas."

Sister Leona, et al, had no idea how many "wrong ideas" I harbored by age sixteen. By that time, I was well along the road of church defined female wrong-headedness. Once the camouflaged roadblocks concealing the "male only" roads were breached by a few intrepid souls who had tired of the forced female march, the gig was up. There was no reason I, or any other woman, couldn't be what we wanted to be. Scores of books later – Simone de Beauvoir, Betty Friedan, Angela Davis, Andrea Dworkin, Elizabeth Cady Stanton, among others – I felt as if I finally understood the elaborate plot that was designed to keep me and my sisters on our knees, wearing dresses, covering our heads with a mantilla, and giving an unqualified, "Yes, Father," or, "Yes, Sir," for the rest of our lives to men who walked with clay feet. And so, garter beltless, but never braless, I forged ahead, armed with my bible and my brain, with a profound understanding that God, as the Apostle Paul wrote, was no respecter of persons. The truth had, indeed, set me free, free to be whatever God wanted me to be I broke loose from the generations of women chained to male definitions of the feminine. I would never look back. No male could ever again claim to be in charge of my life, my body, or my salvation.

You would think that I would go on to lead a most unconventional life, but I didn't. Like many women who came of age during the early days of the Women's Liberation Movement, I wanted to "have it all." I married my high school sweetheart at age 22, and had four children and two foster children. The husband and the kids gave me impeccable Catholic credentials in the Theology of the Body department. But all the while, I remained a rebel, maintaining an uneasy alliance with a church that invariably and painfully let me down. Although my children received their sacraments and I attended church, I wondered how long I could remain a part of an institution that would not allow prepubescent girls, including my own daughter, to be altar servers. Apparently, the dangly parts still mattered.

Always a "plain clothes hippie," I became the same type of adult, a mainstream mom with an attitude. Like Aunt Nellie, I had a nose for hypocrisy. I was 34, and sitting through yet another ill-prepared, inane homily in my parish church, when I turned to my husband and said, "I am leaving and I am never coming back"

We had very close friends who were observant Lutherans. My husband and I met their pastor, his wife, and their three children. For the first time in my life, I actually realized that it was possible and probable that ordained priests/ministers could be both pastors and husbands because the church is in, of, and from the world since it was founded by our Emmanuel, God who lived among us.

I almost took the ultimate *contra legem* step of becoming a Lutheran, but reconsidered. Why would I allow men whose understanding of womanhood was a humble, "undefiled," obedient, sexless, passionless virgin drive me out of a Church that my family most probably belonged to from as far back as the time of St. Bridget? Why not expect, yes, demand that the Church live up to its own best self, the community of believers described by Jesus and Paul, wherein there are no fathers, no humanly defined positions of authority, no male and female roles, because all are one in Christ Jesus?

After meeting Protestant clergy and attending Protestant worship, I also came to realize that there could be many other ways of "doing" church, which God always graces with Divine Presence, for what mere mortal can ever contain or command or control the presence of Almighty God? I learned that there was no magic involved in the ordination process. No special privileges were conferred by celibacy, no "ontological" change occurred with ordination. Good people doing the work of God are good people. Priestly people, those who willingly serve others, are priestly people. The transformative process begins not with a religious rite that directs the Spirit of God from outside, but as God within, who seeps out of the soul, altering us until, as Paul said, it is not we who live, but God, God's very self who lives within us. Once the Spirit of God commandeers the soul, anything is possible. *Contra legem* behavior becomes inevitable.

The gospels and Pauline epistles supply Catholics with a basis for *contra legem* behavior. Jesus, who lived among poor in captive Israel, repeatedly told people to stop and desist from the practice of slavish obedience to rules that prevented the full flourishing of every human being. Paul, the self-described zealous Pharisee, learned to his dismay,

59

as he lay blinded by a bolt of light that knocked him from his horse, that instead of serving God, his violent persecution of the followers of Jesus actually harmed our Emmanuel, God with us and in us. Thus, Paul had to break the law he had written on his heart as a youth, the law that sustained him in adulthood, in order to love God more abundantly and become the person God wanted him to be. Like Jesus, who healed on the Sabbath in direct violation of the law, Paul removed circumcision as an entry requirement for non-Jews who wished to follow Jesus. Both Paul and Jesus minimized dietary restrictions that had become cumbersome for Israel's poor. For Paul, all things were lawful if they worked for the greater glory of God. According to Jesus, the whole of law upon which all other rules and regulations rest is the love of God and love of neighbor as self. As Jesus proved by his life and his death, a Christian must be willing to act *contra legem* whenever laws harm individuals within the Body of Christ.

I honed my experience of God during the seven years I spent in the Lutheran Theological Seminary of Philadelphia, where I was welcomed with open arms, a lone Roman Catholic even though substantial numbers of my classmates were former Catholics – the Roman Catholic Church's loss, a great gain for the denominations that received them. I attended evening classes with people from many different religious denominations: African Methodist Episcopal, Pentecostal, United Church of Christ, Disciples of Christ, United Methodist, Episcopal, Church of God in Christ, Church of South India, and Baptist, as well as Lutheran. My classmates were young and old, black and white, married and single, gay and straight, rich and poor, conservative and liberal, American, African, South American, and Asian. During those seven years, I experienced the continual outpouring of the Spirit who recognizes neither human boundaries nor platonic ideals. What divides Christians from one another is not worth mentioning. It is sin and a lack of faith in God, rather than God's laws, that keep Christians apart. The radical equality of all people before God that Paul preached should determine the nature of our Eucharistic practices. I felt this radical equality, as well as a profound sense of unity with my sisters and brothers, when Protestant pastors stated prior to communion that all were welcome to eat at the table of Jesus Christ.

I learned at seminary that God, the Mother/Father almighty is, was, and will always be bigger than what any religious set of rules and practices can define. The Holy Spirit of God simply cannot be contained, retained, restrained, explained, or maintained by men – or women. God is wild, holy fire, "shook foil," according to poet Gerard Manley Hopkins. Peter, like the prophet Joel, and later Augustine, described the incomprehensible nature of God who pours out God's spirit upon the less than usual suspects. Before Joshua, Moses' successor, understood the depth and breadth and height of God's power, he bitterly complained to Moses about undesignated people prophesizing in the Name of *Ha Shem*, the Lord God. Moses, the great law-giver himself, responded incredulously, "Are you jealous for my sake?" (Numbers 11:29). Jesus received a similar complaint from his disciples when they tried to restrict something Jesus wanted poured out and overflowing into everyone's lap. Jesus, like Moses, dismissed out-of-hand the idea of human controlled parceling out of God's power. God's power simply cannot be limited by man-made rules.

When I entered seminary in 2000, I thought I had no desire for ordination. I told myself and others that I wanted to learn the language that the church uses to oppress women. I have learned that language and speak it well. But here I was in a seminary, pursuing a Master of Divinity, which included courses in preaching, pastoral care, and hospital chaplaincy. Despite my protests to the contrary, my classmates and professors decided that I should be ordained. If I converted and became a Lutheran, they said, I could have a place in the Lutheran Church I could join the ranks of the many thousands of Roman Catholics who have walked away from their church. I could become a Lutheran pastor and work within, rather than outside, the church. My New Testament professor, however, demurred. God, she said, needed people to remain on the outside of institutions – even to the point of excommunication – in order to hold institutions accountable to their mission. She reminded me of the words that echo through the pages of scripture, "Do not fear." To fear, as Howard Thurman wrote, is to deliver oneself to destruction.

I had no idea of what I was going to do until I met Bishop Patricia Fresen in March of 2005 at the Southeastern Pennsylvania Women's Ordination Conference twenty-fifth anniversary celebration. Bishop Patricia invited me to apply for ordination through Roman Catholic Womenpriests. On July 31, 2006, I was ordained a priest against the expressed wishes of the cardinal archbishop of Philadelphia, who in a letter prior to my ordination labeled me a "public scandal," although he had never met me. Two weeks after my ordination, he submitted my name to Rome for excommunication, a reward for my *contra legem* behavior. As of March 26, 2008, I have heard no word from Rome or from the Archdiocese of Philadelphia.

Despite the disapprobation of the bishops who have declared that all sacraments administered by women priests are invalid, a group of people invited me to be their priest. Together, we celebrate the

Eucharist every Sunday in a United Methodist chapel. Like the *basileia* of Jesus, our *contra legem* assembly, The Community of Saint Mary Magdalene, is no respecter of persons. We are a discipleship of equals that welcomes all of God's children to a place where charity and love prevail. Community organized, owned, and operated, it is the People of God who serve each other as priests by virtue of their membership in what Peter called "the priesthood of all believers." As disciples of the living God, we believe that we have been charged to bring the peace of Jesus, the love of God, and the communion of the Holy Spirit to all we meet.

Since I have traveled only a short distance down the road of priesthood, I tread lightly and go slowly. God is so great and the world so awesome. As I push aside the brambles that clog this ancient path, I can see the Lamb in the distance feeding the great multitudes who stream toward the light of his Presence. He smiles, extending the cup and the plate, and announces in a great voice, "Let everyone who hungers and thirsts come to my banquet. How welcome are you all to feast at the table of the living God!"

Ordained a priest: 2006, Pittsburgh

HOW COULD I NOT DO THIS?

A Story of Call to Priesthood
Andrea Johnson

I AM A THIRD GENERATION Italian-American, born and raised a Catholic in Ventnor, New Jersey, USA. I attended Catholic schools, including St. Mary's College, Notre Dame, Indiana, a college of the Sisters of the Holy Cross. My professional education includes a graduate degree in international affairs and diplomacy from the Fletcher School of Law and Diplomacy, Tufts University, Medford, Massachusetts, USA. I have been happily married to Spencer Johnson, now a retired naval officer, for 38 years; we have three grown children: Spencer V (37 years); Melissa (33 years); and Matthew (30 years) as well as two wonderful grandchildren. Our life is rich and full. In being ordained as a Roman Catholic Womanpriest, I am not looking for a profession to fulfill me.

I am a lifelong Catholic, and have served several times over the years as a director of religious education and a secondary level religious education teacher in parishes. From 1983 to 1985, I was parish minister in a priestless parish in rural Virginia, one hour from Washington, DC. This experience was pivotal to the recognition of my call.

Our tradition says that God calls people to serve the community of believers. In the Hebrew Scriptures, there are the stories of Moses, Samuel, Jeremiah, David and Elijah. We hear of the mysterious voice of God, and often of signs and wonders. In the Christian Testament, we have the call of Mary and the call of Jesus, as well as the call of Saul, renamed Paul. Again, we see signs and wonders. But then, we also have the call of each of the Twelve – a simple, "Come, follow me;" and there is the call to the Gentiles to be church – a heated discussion and a contested decision, to be sure! In this case, God seemed to rely on the wisdom of the community.

It was in a similar fashion that I experienced my call to ordination. It was quite unexpected, to say the least. I had never thought about it as a child. It did not start out as a "Jesus and me" experience. Having spent many years as a catechist, I was hired by an Army post chapel to coordinate parish ministries for the Catholic congregation. The parish had lost its Catholic chaplain's billet, and depended upon contract priests from Washington for sacraments. The parish was fairly conservative and very Mass-oriented, and was distraught at the loss. Needless to say, they were less than enthralled at my arrival and the new arrangements. I was now the on-site, day in, day out parish minister. The priest traveled an hour to be with us for four hours a week. I started out to do the best job of "coordination" that I could.

The process very quickly revealed itself to be a mammoth community-building project. A parish council was formed and empowered. People trained in great numbers for liturgical and education ministries. Adult education and spirituality programs took off. In six months' time, the community had bonded. The priests who came on Sundays were happily drawn into the circle. A new way of being the Vint Hill Catholic Chapel community came into being.

It was at this point that I began to ponder the incongruity of the situation. Why was it necessary for us to cobble together such a compartmentalized parish ministry for such a small parish? Why couldn't a woman or a married man be the sacramental minister as well as the "coordinator" of ministries? I began to pursue theological studies, and to prayerfully reflect on the disconnect between the realities which my priest colleagues and I were living with versus the needs of the community. For my part, I did not feel that I was in control of all that was happening. I felt stretched in doing this work, but I was happy to be stretched. I felt a part of something very creative. The community's response led me to understand my call. It was their interaction with me that called forth the reflection which allowed me to hear the voice of God.

In 1985, our family moved to Japan because of my husband's orders to assume the position of Commander Destroyer Squadron 15, Yokosuka. Over the ensuing years, both in Japan and afterwards, I continued to participate in pastoral ministries in many places and many milieus, including at St. Andrew by the Bay Church, my present parish in Annapolis, Maryland. My "day jobs" during the twenty years between my leaving my parish coordinator position and my admission to the RCWP formation program for priesthood included a number of years as a program officer at the Senior Fulbright Scholars Program in Washington, DC, as well as four years as the executive director of the Women's Ordination Conference. I have thoroughly enjoyed my professional life as well as my role as spouse and parent. They are an integral part of who I am. My call to priesthood encompasses all of those aspects of who I am. In my view, priests are not called to be "cookie cutter" Christians any more than any other Christian called by God to any ministry among the People of God.

Another important element convincing me of my call to priesthood was my deep sense that the only voice, the only face of God that was being experienced by Catholic believers at liturgy was that of a male. My experience with our small Army parish impressed upon me the hunger that people felt for a feminine face and voice of God. I thought about the face of centralized power in a pyramidal Catholic Church, and how non-life-giving that was for the people. Was the voice of the Holy Spirit being stifled in the Church?

In fact, when one observes the many signs of retrenchment vis-à-vis the progress made by Vatican Council II, and the creeping triumphalism which seems to be dominating recent teachings and pronouncements from the Vatican, it is tempting to say that the Holy Spirit has too little room in the Church. It is undeniable that there are places in the Church where the Spirit appears to have no maneuvering room, where things are locked down for the sake of good order and prevention of scandal. Thinking, dialogue and growth in understanding are very unpopular activities in the Roman dicasteries, in many diocesan chanceries and at episcopal synods. This pervasive attitude of retrenchment is reflected in contemporary readings of canon law and of the church's catechism. Lock-down, uniformity are the order of the day. The Spirit indeed has no room. The Spirit apparently has no voice at the center of ecclesial power. She is crowded out by priorities concerned with maintaining *unbroken traditions* and leaving nothing to "chance."

Ideally, the center of ecclesial power should be deeply spiritual, that is Spirit-filled. The question is: Is the center of ecclesial power really spiritual in nature? Or is it temporal power masquerading as spiritual power? Do the fruits of the exercise of this power resemble what we know from Scripture about the fruits of the Spirit? Sadly, no.

On the other hand, there are, I believe, places within the Church where the Spirit does have room to fill and to nurture the Church, and to cause it to grow in wisdom and grace. Those places are not at the center of power, but rather at the margins, among people who, because they are oppressed or poor, are not blinded by the notion that all is well and that the Church should be about the business of maintaining the status quo (or the *unbroken tradition*). The Spirit also has room among the compassionate, those who are able to put themselves in the place of the marginalized, those who know they have much to learn and much spiritual growing to do. These compassionate ones seek to break down barriers; they place real people's needs over the demands of onerous laws. The Spirit has plenty of room among those at the margins whose priorities are justice, mercy and peace; and also among those whose lives are uncluttered, who can see and hear and read the signs of the times.

The way I see it, our arduous task as Roman Catholic Womenpriests is to work to bring the spiritual power generated at the margins of the Church to bear on the center. We have been told in the Book of Exodus that Ruach will lead us, a cloud by day and a pillar of fire by night. We womenpriests, as *worker priests,* can perhaps listen and learn at the margins, and gather the Spirit's wisdom in order to birth *a new kind of priesthood that remains dependent upon the margins* and refuses to go into lock-down mode, squeezing out the Spirit of God.

When the possibility of Roman Catholic ordination through the Roman Catholic Womenpriests group became an option in 2002, I began to discern my response. I made many attempts to run away from or put off a decision to proceed. Indeed, this is not a decision I made impulsively, or without a great deal of input from many people with whom I have ministered, people I respect deeply. I have understood that the Spirit has been leading me, preparing me, and finally calling me, through the various people in my faith communities over the years. I have concluded that I am called to do this. I will minister with people who feel themselves marginalized or alienated from the institutional church for whatever reason. It is what God asks of me. The discernment process has been prayerful, lengthy, gut-wrenching at times – but the conclusion has been indisputable.

I understand that obedience to God's call comes at a great cost. Canon 1024 states: *A baptized male alone receives sacred ordination validly.* Competent Catholic scripture scholars and theologians find no scriptural or divine law that prevent a woman from being ordained. As a matter of fact, history and archaeology reveal examples of ordained women in the early church. The history of this canon has been traced not to God's will nor to Jesus' intent, but to culturally and time-limited understandings of the basic nature of women and of men.

In obedience to the gospel of Jesus Christ, I have now disobeyed this unjust law, Canon 1024, through valid but illicit ordination as a Roman Catholic woman priest during the summer of 2007. Given the overwhelming reasons to stand for justice, how could I not do this?

The validity of these Roman Catholic Womenpriests ordinations is, of course, the central issue. The women bishops who ordain women priests and deacons have been validly ordained by male bishops in good standing with the Vatican. We believe there is no question regarding the validity of orders, but they are indeed illicit, with the specific intent to bring about a change to Canon 1024.

I, like the others ordained in our initiative, do not intend to start a church. Although I may face interdict or excommunication as a result of my action, I remain a Roman Catholic. I will exercise my priesthood by reaching out to those people in the margins, the apathetic ones, the hurt ones, the excluded ones – and minister to them. I will encourage them to become active in the parishes, and in the spirit of Vatican II, to use their voices in renewing the church. I will encourage them to serve the poor, and to work for social justice.

This is who I am, and why I have been ordained. This is why other faithful Catholics support my ordination.

Ordained a priest: 2007, New York

DRAW ME, WE SHALL RUN*

Gabriella Velardi Ward

I HAVE HEARD SPIRIT CALL me from the time I was a five-year old child. Spirit showed herself to me in the darkened, incense-filled church as we chanted during Benediction. Spirit showed herself to me in the mystery and symbolism of the Mass during Eucharist. Spirit showed herself to me when I was alone and afraid.

I was very close to Jesus, Mary and the saints as a child. They were my friends and companions. Since I was also drawn toward art, I began to draw chalices and monstrances, tabernacles and vestments. And so it was very natural that, at the age of five, I would say that I wanted to be a priest when I grew up.

Throughout my many years in ministry, I have felt that I was a priest, even though I was not formally ordained. People began to look to me as a spiritual leader, asking for guidance and confiding in me their deepest secrets.

I have, at times, felt Spirit move through me while I was performing my ministry. At times, I have been driven to my knees in gratitude to God for what happened during a counseling session, and for being allowed to be a part of it. For the last twelve years, I have spiritually companioned and counseled adult survivors of child abuse.

My ministry began to take form in 1994 when I was teaching meditation based on the work of Anthony deMello, SJ. Before long, people began to ask to speak to me after the night's meditation. Many of them were dealing with child abuse issues, physical, sexual and emotional.

I had spent a number of years, by then, studying the work of Alice Miller, a German psychotherapist who has written extensively on child abuse. I soon realized that the combination of Anthony deMello and Alice Miller worked well to help survivors process the trauma from their bodies. Alice Miller said that, in order to get through the trauma, one needs to experience the feelings that were disconnected at the time of the traumatic event. Through his awareness exercises, Anthony deMello tells one how to reconnect those feelings. From this realization, I developed techniques to help survivors process their memories.

As my study went deeper into the psychological, social and religious aspects of this systemic problem, I began exploring these issues in my writings. I explored such topics as "The Theological Implications of Child Sexual Abuse" and "Sin, Conversion and Reconciliation When Survivors are the Context."

I would like to explain what I have learned, in my ministry, of the process of sin, conversion and reconciliation in light of child abuse. I feel that it is important for those who companion survivors, including priests, as well as those who love survivors, to understand the inner life of survivors.

Sin, Conversion and Reconciliation

As children, when we learned the answers to the questions in the Baltimore Catechism – answers about God and sin – there was no ambiguity, no doubt, and no context to those questions. There was something comforting in knowing so surely the answers. While surety may also be comforting to an adult, there is something wonderful about paradox, ambiguity, and lack of certainty.

Growth is generally the outcome when we struggle with the answers to God and life questions, and when we search for the answers in the context of the time and culture in which we live. Further growth is experienced when we grapple with the stories of our individual lives and apply them to the search for God. It forces our horizon, our limits, to expand. It opens our mind to possibilities. And it helps us accept the gift of difference.

When we look at the interrupted lives of those who have experienced trauma stemming from child abuse, sin, conversion and reconciliation take on a different meaning. The resultant mental and emotional illness, the compulsions, addictions, and violence turned inward or outward, needs also to be put into context. So the concept of sin as stated in the Baltimore Catechism is not so simple after all. The understanding, for survivors, of the brokenness of their lives (sin), how they achieve change (conversion), and the way they make things right again (repentance and reconciliation), is a process unlike what we have been taught.

Human beings are born to be relational. Children need relationship in order to survive. When the child sees in the eyes of the adult love and care, the child will thrive. But if the child sees in the eyes of the adult lack of value, and experiences neglect, deprivation and physical or sexual abuse, that child grows in isolation, unable to form bonds, mistrusting self and the world around her/him.

What is learned from the abuse is that it is permissible for the stronger to dominate the weaker and more vulnerable. Power means power over. That child learns that getting one's needs met is more important than not harming another.

The tragic consequences of abuse and neglect are loss of self, loss of capacity for empathy, compassion, mutuality, and the ability to give and receive unconditional love. It becomes impossible for the child to form strong bonds, which are desperately needed for growth and health. The ability to be relational is shattered and remains a problem throughout life.

Children are geniuses at finding ways to survive. Sometimes, since it is too painful or too threatening to blame the adult who should be loving and nurturing, they blame themselves. Guilt and shame result. Sometimes, they find a way to disconnect from the trauma by dissociating. Sometimes, they become super achievers and sometimes they express their pain through acting out violently. These survival techniques follow them into adulthood, and while they may have helped the child survive, these techniques become a problem for the adult that child becomes.

Long after the abuse or trauma has stopped, the agony continues and affects all areas of the victim's life, psychologically, physically, spiritually, intellectually, and socially. The result is tremendous disconnection from the world that wrecks havoc on their bodies, minds and spirits. Overcoming this handicap is no easy feat. The victim stays a victim long after the abuse has stopped. Everything is colored by the fact of the abuse. It is only after experiencing much psychic and physical pain that the victim may begin to recover the gift of life.

Victims of child abuse, as well as other traumatic events, may develop Post Traumatic Stress Disorder (PTSD). The effects of PTSD can be nightmares, flashbacks, dissociative behavior, easy startle response, hyper vigilance, eating disorders, and the inability to form and keep relationships, especially healthy ones. If the memories are not processed, the outcome can be violence directed against oneself or against society.

If not processed, these painful experiences can breed anger, hatred, depression, and rage toward self, others, nature, and God. Survivors also experience fear, powerlessness, isolation, exploitation, and confusion of sexual identity, fear of intimacy, low self-esteem, loss of a sense of personhood, an exaggerated sense of responsibility, as well as destructive behavior. They may spend a lifetime learning how to keep themselves safe, and may never succeed. They may struggle with the idea of trust of self, of others, especially of those in authority, and ultimately of God.

Some statistics concerning child abuse can be enlightening. One in three girls and one in seven boys is sexually abused as a child. Eighty-five percent of alcoholics, drug addicts and prostitutes and 90 percent of people in jail were abused as children. Ninety percent of survivors have eating disorders 90 percent have depressive disorder, 75 percent consider suicide, 40 percent attempt suicide, and 15 percent commit suicide.[5]

God's grace is always given and can overcome any condition, but a failure to take the effects of the conditions spoken of above into account when sin, conversion and reconciliation are considered, and a failure on the part of the healer or priest, if reconciliation is to be sacramental, to heal his or her own life, may hinder the ability to mediate God's healing and forgiving grace. It may also hinder the seeker of God's grace to receive it.

Sin, Conversion and Reconciliation Revisited

Sin never happens in a vacuum. There is always context, and the context is the pain of our lives. From the discussion above, one can see that sin is the making of wrong choices from unresolved pain. Sometimes those choices are not even made consciously. And sometimes a person, if addicted, is compelled to make those wrong choices. There is, in those cases, a lack of freedom.

Some theologians have called sin pride, self-assertion and rebellion against God. Some have said sin is any deliberate infidelity to the will of God. And some state that serious sin occurs when the refusal to do God's will is a free, conscious and radical decision.

Is it, therefore, a sin when the "sin" is not deliberate, or when there is no free or conscious decision, as in compulsions and addictions? Who defines the will of God? The definitions of sin and God's will have been developed by men in cultures that encourage them to roles of domination, authority and privilege. The concept of willful rebellion against God comes from a lack of understanding of the broken relationship and lack of trust in God that can happen as a result of trauma and oppression. A feminist understanding of God's will must be God's preference for the liberation of the individual and a preference

---

[5] Statistics are taken from the work of Renee Fredrickson, PhD, Ave Clark, O.P., Alice Miller and Judith Herman, MD.

for freedom from that which prevents one from being fully human and fully alive.

We were told, as children, that anger is a cardinal sin. It is not. Anger is an emotion that tells you something is wrong. What you do with that anger may be the wrong choice made from pain. Denial of anger for fear of committing a "sin" may allow oppression to continue, and may be used to keep the oppressed, including women, under control. Anger internalized may become self-destructive. Anger denied may end in violence.

How is gluttony a sin when seen in the light of the statistics stated above, when 90 percent of survivors have eating disorders – food addictions, obesity, anorexia or bulimia – and 85 percent are addicted to drugs and alcohol? And how is it a sin when survivors use these substances to self-medicate, to ease their pain? Certainly, these are questions with which we need to grapple.

We were told that pride is a sin. One can see how that understanding can come from the experience of those in power and of a privileged class. What happens when one is forced to be "humble," when one is forced to be vulnerable, dependent or weak? What happens when one is forced to not acknowledge the talents God has given? What does this do to one's self-image? A feminist understanding of humility is the ability to walk in truth. If you are good at something, you acknowledge it. That is humility. If you are not good at something you acknowledge that too. That is also humility.

For survivors of trauma, especially those of child abuse, pride may be a sign of growth, of pride in oneself and one's accomplishments. In other words, pride may be the evidence of getting healthy. Pride may be the accomplishment of self-assertion and the discovery of one's personhood.

I do not have statistics on the struggle with underachievement and poverty in relationship to survivors of trauma. From my experience, a good number of people struggle with money, housing, and poverty as a direct result of what they have experienced. This is quite evident in the large percentage of homeless who are survivors or veterans of war. It has to become clear that the struggle of survivors to become financially independent is not avarice or greed, even if that struggle becomes a consuming issue.

The issue of lust is also a tricky one for survivors, especially of sexual abuse. Control over one's body was taken away from the survivor. There may be a confusion of sex and love in one who has experienced this kind of violation so young. The survivor may use sex as a way of exercising control over the gender that had been the abuser.

And the high statistics of those survivors who become prostitutes is evidence that more is going on than meets the eye. Growth for these survivors may be the ability to love one's body and sexuality and to connect to another in a loving physical and safe way.

I won't belabor the point with the cardinal sins of envy and sloth. But the same kind of thinking can be applied to those behaviors as well. It is also interesting to note that the seven cardinal sins do not include murder. An historical, social and political analysis of that might be interesting, as well as useful. The point is that the symptoms of trauma and oppression are not sins. Even the acting out of those symptoms may not be sins since there is a lack of awareness and a lack of freedom.

In order to bring survivors to the point of looking at the brokenness in their lives and begin to achieve change, the survivors must feel safe. They cannot even begin to feel safe if they do not have a safe place and a safe person with which to process that brokenness. For conversion to happen, the survivor needs to look at the original cause.

Sometimes it takes God's infinite grace in order to be able to overcome the fear and pain of things buried so deeply and to look at them. This grace is part of the process of conversion. Through grace, the survivors begin to see the cause of their pain, and with the help of a safe and understanding person, begin to heal their broken lives.

Redemptive grace gives survivors the courage it takes to seek healing work, to touch the feelings of anger and grief, and to enter into a process of restoring authentic relationship by setting their voices free. The healing of wounds and refusal to allow the suffering and loss to be the final word are also works of grace. The work of the priest or spiritual guide is to aid in this process by being a non-judgmental, accepting and safe presence in order to mediate that grace.

Reconciliation with self, the world and God happens when survivors takes steps toward empowerment, justice and the re-creation of self as they work against suffering. Reconciliation happens when survivors can begin to feel authentically, truthfully, the feelings that may include anger and the pain of becoming visible. Reconciliation happens when they begin to break the conspiracy of silence and reclaim their truth.

By confronting the lies, the silences, the distortions and manipulations, they do the work of God. By allowing holy anger against those who would corrupt a child's body as the temple of God's Spirit, they move toward recovering their lives. As they begin to trust in God, they begin to understand God's infinite capacity for loving relationship.

When they acknowledge and trust their feelings and perceptions, their lives open to a whole new significance. When, in the company of God, they can turn and face their fears and chase them down, their fears will no longer interfere with their lives. Then their lives will be made right. Then they will be reconciled to themselves, the world and God.

Stepping Out

I earn my living as an architect and artist. I am a spiritual director. My course of study in the Seminary included the psychology of spirituality and Ignatian and Carmelite Spirituality. Continuing independent study includes many alternative methods of healing, such as meditation, psycho-spiritual breath work, family constellation therapy, bio-spirituality through focusing, the visualizations of Anthony deMello and Belleruth Naparstek. I have also taught meditation since 1993 and have spent many years in parish ministries.

I look forward to the day when, as a priest, I can lead a reconciliation service for survivors of trauma. I look forward to the day when I can be part of the mediation of God's grace in a sacramental way, and I look foreword to the day when I can make manifest the bread of desire and the body of love that is the Eucharist.

The question was asked: What motivates me to step out and act *contra legem*, to accept a valid ordination if not a licit one? At this point in my life, there are two reasons. The first is the failure of the institutional church to protect children from assault by priests and the subsequent cover-up by the institutional bishops, the failure of the institution to hear the voices of survivors and the failure of the institution to understand, with compassion, the pain involved in trying to put the pieces of one's life back together.

The second motivating factor was a talk given by Patricia Fresen, validly ordained bishop in the RCWP movement. In it, she discussed the modeling of a non-hierarchical and inclusive Roman Catholic Church. I, like the others in the movement, love the Roman Catholic Church. I love the sacramental nature of the rituals, the history and tradition of mysticism, and the history of social justice activism. To have that as well as a non-hierarchical structure and an inclusive church, seems closer to what the original founder had envisioned.

Through the years, I have had the opportunity to be ordained to the priesthood in a number of alternative ways. But they never felt right. When I found RCWP, I felt that this is where my call to the priesthood, heard as a child and again in my adult life, would be fulfilled.

Many have asked me how my intense interest on this subject came about. The answer is, yes, I am a survivor, a wounded healer, if you will. In the quote from Therese of Lisieux that I titled this essay with, she refers to herself as a current, a body of water, being drawn toward God. But in the body of water many elements, stones, sand, branches are also drawn along with the current. She referred to these elements as the souls she would bring along with her as she moved toward God.

I also feel that God has drawn me, leading me to all the methods I have used to heal the trauma that I have experienced. And in the wake of my current, I in turn, draw other souls toward God.

*Therese of Lisieux, *Story of a Soul*

Ordained a priest: 2008, Boston

Judith A. B. Lee, Priest
Eleonora Marinaro, Priest
Bridget Mary Meehan, Priest
Janice Sevre-Duszynska, Priest

Judy Lee presides at Church in the Park, a ministry to the Homeless in Ft. Myers, Florida

Bridget Mary Meehan presides at liturgy at Mary, Mother of Jesus, House Church in Sarasota, Florida

A PRIEST OF THE POOR

Judith A. B. Lee

M Y CALL TO THE priesthood has evolved as a strongly growing call within my lifelong call to serve as Jesus did. For me this means sacramental ministry with the poor, the ill, the different, and the outcasts of society by virtue of color, caste, sexual orientation, mental or physical illnesses or challenges.

While I have always served, in 2006 I began to set all other things aside to fully discern and enact the call. Early in 2007 I met Bridget Mary Meehan, RCWP, at a house Mass. This was a providential meeting of grace and understanding that plunged me deeper into discernment and service. I continued my work with several families from a mission parish and my own parish, and I returned to my work with those at the very bottom – the homeless and the hungry – in an outdoor feeding ministry initially started by a Lutheran-Episcopal church. It became clear to me that serving my wounded people as a priest with the renewed and inclusive Roman Catholic Women Priests was the road I was called to take.

My vision of ministry was shaped by the love of Jesus as I experienced it in human faces and arms throughout the years. Some of those arms have embraced me and sent me forth, and others have, in their pain, reached out to be lifted up, but all are the presence of Christ. My vision is strongly influenced by the Holy Scriptures and empowered by the Spirit of G^d/Godde.*

For me, the question is more "Who" than "what" called me to serve the poor, for the work is sometimes so hard that I would run from it if not for Godde's call. The voice within calls clearly. I hear it sometimes in the night, and when standing in awe of creation as with Moses in the mountains. I hear it by the sea with the disciples, and in community (*ekklesia/* "church") with Mary and Martha and Mary of Magdala. A fire grows in my heart and belly. It is a passion for that which I am called to do. Like Moses, it includes a call from Godde's heart to my own. "I have felt their sufferings," says G^d (Ex 3:7). And

I feel them, and am almost consumed by them. G^d's people become my people. I am one with them. I am prepared to serve. Yet, like Moses, I protest that I cannot possibly do this *now*.

My early life experiences and later professional training in social work, counseling, theology and ministry equipped me to serve. I was called to love and follow Jesus as a child at my faith-full grandmother's knee. We were poor, living in an inner-city, richly multicultural Brooklyn neighborhood. With white flight, it became a black neighborhood, having the presence of a strong church and wonderful pastors and youth group leaders. The mental illness, alcoholism, and poverty in the midst of strength and beauty, both in my own family and in the families of friends, gave me empathy and understanding. Following Pastor Melvin G. Williams, I became a professional social worker, and later a professor and theoretician of social work. I served, taught, and wrote about issues of injustice, and felt a passion for the poor. But there was always a piece missing. I had a pastor's call, but not yet within the Church.

As I moved up in academia, I began to become distanced from the poor. I also moved away from the church, as it moved away from me when I accepted and owned the complexity of my sexuality, painfully left a marriage and, though androgynous, eventually lived with a woman, accepting the stigma and shunning of an open life. I lived as a border dweller, and sometimes an outcast who, come what may, continued to love Jesus.

Then, in the early 1980's, Godde guided my steps daily through Washington Square Park on my way to teach at NYU. There the modern-day "wretched of the earth" slept on the park benches and froze in winter. I began to engage these lonely people in dialogue. I could not sleep. I got up and read the Scriptures. Matthew 25 and Isaiah 58 were open before me. The pages burned as I touched them. I knew that G^d was calling me, also an outcast, to serve the poorest of the poor. I told Godde that I didn't know if I could do it, and that I was a strange choice! Still I said "yes." The next day, I wrote a proposal, and entered the city shelters for women and began my work on many levels. As I moved among the broken women of all sorts in a 150-bed shelter, I looked into their eyes and immediately recognized that social work intervention could not touch lives here, but G^d's love would. I would bring love and prayer as much as I would bring my skills. I was blessed in serving. I continued this work in Connecticut, and later in Guyana, South America. It shaped the rest of my life in many unforeseen ways.

I wrestled with the call again in the early part of 2007, as I realized that G^d was making a way for ordination as a Roman Catholic woman priest. This was not a "general call," but specifically so that I could serve the poor, the stranger in the land, and the outcast. I was more than ready to prepare for and move on toward ordination, but a part of me wanted to keep this separate from serving G^d's blessed and sometimes difficult people. I told G^d that I was too old for this kind of work, that I had given much of my life to it and it was time to rest. I argued that southwest Florida, this right-wing playground of the rich, is the last place it could be done as there are no resources or support. There is no fire for the poor unless it is to consume them. I told Jesus that loving G^d's precious broken people would hurt too much. (How could I ever say that to Jesus, who gave all, and to the Christ who appears before me in their faces?) I told G^d that I did not need to add a thick outer layer to my feelings about life's losses and unfair changes. I wrestled with Jesus over taking the cup. And finally, I was sick of academic work, and did not want to research or write another paper in my life. I pushed back at the Spirit who pushed and pulled me with love into the work. I know that G^d was as sick of me as YHWH was of Moses with all his excuses. So G^d gave me an "Aaron" for support, two or three, and more…many more. I was blessed with a wise, courageous, wonderful RCWP mentor in Bridget Mary; with a strong, insightful, caring ministry mentor in Rev. Becky Robbins-Penniman, an Episcopal priest; and by my side supporting me in the work was Joe Irvin, a Corpus priest. I recognized that Godde had provided what I would need to answer the call. Is this not a miracle?

My call is to live in imitation of Christ through G^d's grace and the power of the Holy Spirit. Jesus' authority was to teach and heal, to forgive sins, and to restore the community (Mt 7:29; 9:6; 21:23-27; Crosby, pp.7-8). Restoring the community, by definition, includes justice for the poor. The reign of G^d that Jesus brings is "composed of people who 'sell' their power, possessions, and prestige in such a manner that they enable conditions of powerlessness, poverty, and depression in others to be alleviated" through preaching, healing, teaching, and inviting others to join in this process (Crosby, p.49). This is my call, my ministry, and my intention.

Our alliance with the poor relates strongly to the restoration of the Church, the community of believers. Hence the inclusive renewed Roman Catholic priesthood holds the poor and oppressed to its very heart. The equality of women as priests must symbolize the equality of all who suffer as second class, both within and outside of the institutional Church.

The Good News comes first to the poor, who are beloved of G^d and fed, nourished and empowered by that love to live and flourish

79

with dignity, and to overthrow the systems that exploit and oppress. In this struggle, which is actually a class struggle, G^d clearly and strongly takes the side of the poor. This does not mean that G^d does not love all G^d's children, but that when some exploit and hurt and oppress others, G^d is on the side of the exploited, not the exploiter (Brown, pp.33-39).

G^d calls us to join in the struggle. G^d does not "enlighten the powerful but empowers the powerless," and this is very good news to the powerless (Brown, p.43). Jesus shouts this news again from the mountainside to G^d's poor: "Congratulations, you poor, for yours is the kingdom (reign) of God" (Mt 5:3, *Scholars Translation*).

We women have led, despite our own oppression, in the liberation of the poor and exploited and this assists in the birth of G^d's people. Mary announced G^ds's priority and Jesus' mission to the poor: "You have deposed the mighty from their thrones and raised the lowly to high places. You have filled the hungry with good things." (Lk 1:52-53, *The Inclusive Bible: The First Egalitarian Translation*). The exodus story (Ex 1:8-14;2:23-25;3:7-10) shows the particular role of women (vv.15-22) in the struggle for liberation. The Hebrew midwives cleverly trick Pharaoh and assist in the birth of G^d's people. Even so, we as Roman Catholic women priests are risking "Pharaoh's" wrath to assure that the Church is continually reborn – alive and healthy. We work for justice so that life is not drained out of G^d's people by male power and domination, and the oppression of women, the poor and other powerless groups.

Jesus turns the world upside down, and his message and life are full of the unexpected – surprises that can change everything (Brown). The unexpected good news for the poor has two central intertwined themes: Jesus as Healer and Jesus as Liberator. The Scriptures see poverty as rooted in oppression (de Garcia and Johnson). Oppression and poverty can bend and break people. Illness of body, mind and soul that flourishes in poverty has existed throughout time. It is my prayer that my ministry will also bring healing and liberation.

Elizabeth Johnson (pp.265-269) sees Christ as Sophia/Wisdom's child. She sees Spirit-Sophia herself as with and for the world, the Three-in-One is suffering with us in "compassion poured out." But this is not an image of a suffering G^d who is powerless, but a G^d who embodies power in love – and thereby empowers us to act to change the suffering we witness and experience. It is the "liberating power of connectedness that is effective in compassionate love" (p. 270). Harrison reminds us that love is not made of soppy stuff in the presence of injustice. Love is "the power to act-each-other-into-well-being"(p.11). The "power of indignation" – to "rage against the dying of the light" – is "the root of the power of love"(p.21). It is cause for indignation to witness the continued suffering of America's homeless people. We are called to radical love as disciples of Jesus. Johnson acknowledges the need to overcome suffering and evil. She says: "...toward that end, speaking about suffering Sophia-God of powerful compassionate love serves as an ally of resistance and a wellspring of hope" (p.272). She places this in the context of Godde's breath/Breath/Holy Spirit, that which sustains me in my work.

In the early Church, the Spirit was seen as a "merciful mother spreading her wings over our sinful times" (Johnson, p.86). Wisdom is manifest as a "street preacher" in Proverbs 1:20-33. I too, with the Spirit's help, am a street preacher – working, worshiping and calling it like it is outside in a park, speaking to and for, and most importantly with, the poor. Perhaps it is also with the spirit of Joanna the Baptist – preparing the way of our G^d for the reign of justice and the kin-dom to come – here, now and forever.

In Proverbs, Sophia is a giver of life and a tree of life. Her words are truth. She is street preacher, life-giver, agent of justice, architect of creation, and G^d's darling, among other roles. Her constant effort is to lure human beings to life (p.88). In the Hebrew Scriptures, G^d is seen as a Mother-Sophia who creates, loves, protects, like a bear robbed of her cubs. Johnson combines feminist theology with liberation theology and ecological and nuclear exigencies (p.183). I agree. My ministry is a Magnificat ministry, and an Isaiah 58 and Matthew 25 ministry: to lift the lowly, feed the hungry and shelter the stranger and the homeless, to free the oppressed. It is ultimately "to bring Good News to those who are poor and proclaim the year of God's favor" (Lk 4:18-20, *TIB*). "The love of God for the world is revealed through the depths of love human beings can feel for one another. We seek and are found by Spirit in the person-creating give and take of loving relationships, in each fresh, particular discovery of the other's beauty"(Johnson, p.125). I have been called to love the poor.

I bring a heart and a spirit that can only be filled by Godde. I bring my radical love, a passion for justice, and a desire to follow Jesus who showed us how to bring the reign of G^d on earth. Formally, I bring theological and ministerial study with a Doctor of Ministry Degree from Global Ministries University and the guidance of qualified mentors that I add to my Doctor of Social Welfare Degree from Yeshiva University and a Masters of Science Degree from Columbia University School of Social Work. I am *Professor Emerita* at the University of Connecticut School of Social Work A Full Professor for many years, I bring twenty-seven years of teaching social work on all levels. This includes mentoring divinity and ministerial students from Yale Divinity School, and clergy and religious from various places; forty-plus years of social work and clinical counseling practice, and decades of parish work with youth, families, and visitation ministry. I also offer the books, articles, and poetry that I have written and published to the service of the kin-dom (for example, Lee, 2001).

As I write this, The Church In The Park is one-year old and we are blessed with amazing growth.

I have been called by a diverse local community, and supported by that community and by my communities throughout the United States and internationally. One of the pastors of my youth, David Ver Nooy, and peers of that group are with me still. In September of 2007, they gathered in a New York church and laid hands on me, praying for the Spirit's indwelling for this journey. Joe Irvin co-pastors with me, and I deeply appreciate his ongoing presence. The Lamb of God Lutheran-Episcopal Congregation, and two prophetic and inspiring pastors – Walter Fohs and Becky Robbins-Penniman – working in a discipleship of equals, emerged to support and co-sponsor The Church In The Park. G^d miraculously restored my life companion, Judy Beaumont, a former Benedictine Sister, after a battle with a rare Leukemia, and she shares in my work fully with different and much needed gifts. And there are more than forty volunteers for the Friday night ministry. (They are from Lamb of God Church, Call To Action of SW Florida, some Catholic parishes, and dear interfaith friends like Stella Odie-Ali and Doreen Sookdeo, and others.) We implement a feeding and worship program, now serving almost one hundred people a week, which includes ministry on all levels of material and spiritual needs. And every week we experience the miracle of the loaves and fishes, as the crowd swells and still we have just enough prepared by many loving hands. I am filled with thanksgiving.

Each week, as I lead the worship service in the park, a core group of "elders" surround me. I stop before the reading of the Gospel. I look around at the rainbow of broken, yet hopeful faces and our eyes meet. I see the grungy clutter of the city park, the cars speeding by with great noise, the children on the swings, the men playing basketball behind us, the smells of a warm dinner and yesterday's beer spilled on the tables and ground permeating the air. I ask, "Where are we standing?" The people respond, "On Holy Ground!" We then chant the hymn "This is Holy Ground, I'm standing on Holy Ground, for G^d is present and where G^d is Holy!" The very ground we stand on is holy. The Breath of the Holy Spirit claims and purifies it, in the same way our very lives are claimed. So the fire in my heart continues, and the Spirit still speaks to the church, and to this servant.

Here is an example of an interactive homily that shows response.

I welcomed them in the Name of God our Mother and Father, and Jesus who shows us how to love, this Easter Vigil evening. I explained what an Easter Vigil is, and how Jesus in the tomb is symbolized by the cross, shrouded in black cloth. I recognized that everyone here has been on the cross of suffering and shame with Jesus. I asked them to help me tell the Good Friday story. (I am using a dialogical style to ask for their stories, their words.) Johnny said the cross was execution. He shared a terrifying experience from the war. He suggested that Ken share too. Ken said he was tortured and almost died in the war, he could understand what Jesus went through on the cross. Ken knew the Scriptures and led us through the words from the cross. Gary said his cross is that his creativity was robbed by the war and he couldn't get back on his feet.

When all had spoken, I asked Bob to read the Scripture. All listened attentively. I named each man by name and pointed to each woman by name and said, "Son, Bob, behold your mother, Ruby. Ruby, behold your son, Bob," all the way around, including the volunteers and myself. "I am looking at my sons, you are looking at your mother, and your sister. And I am looking at my mother, daughters and sisters." (I was putting all of us into the story.) They were into it. Then, I asked what Jesus was saying to us in these words from the cross? Roger said, "He means we are family for each other." Ken added, "and we need to love each other, and not hurt each other anymore." Silence. I agreed, adding that we can be Jesus' love for each other. I asked what Jesus' death and resurrection mean to us? The answers: "It brings hope...hope of getting up off the ground...hope of living again...."

Then we all covered our eyes to experience darkness. Johnny said, "This part is sad, I can do this part. I can't do anything happy." Touching his hand, I said, "In our darkness, let us recall the pain and suffering, hunger and tiredness, longing for a place to lay our heads, sadness and grief, anger and hurt, betrayals and disappointments we carry in our darkness. Let us nail them on the cross with Jesus and bury them in the tomb." Many named what they nailed to the cross. I was deeply touched. Mary was crying and men were wiping their eyes. I then prayed with them that G^d would "lift this darkness from us and raise us from the tomb to new life with Jesus...Amen!" I said. "Now uncover your eyes, let in the Light, it is Easter, we are risen from the dead with Jesus! Jesus lives! We live! Rise up and live!" There were emotional expressions: "Yeah, Amen...Tell it!" as we all did this. (The centrality of resurrection to our faith was poignantly clear.) I took the glass cross out of its shroud and set it high on the table. I asked Roger to light the candle behind it. Everyone cheered.

I have written here of my call to serve G^d's people at Love's Table of Plenty where all are welcome – to break open the precious sacraments for those who hunger and thirst for them, especially those experiencing injustice, poverty, illness and oppression (Ross). We, as women in the Church, are offered only six sacraments, and if we deny our call to serve as priests in sacramental ministry we consent to our own oppression. We are also consenting to the oppression of all of our sisters and brothers in poverty. I could not in conscience consent any longer. The social teachings and primacy of conscience are two of the best-kept secrets in the Church. In embracing these imperatives of Vatican II, I am doing what I must do to serve G^d's people. I thank Godde for the courageous women and men who have preceded me in this, and reach my hand back for those who will join us in renewing the Church in radical love.

* I note here that I use Godde in a familiar sense with a female presence and G^d to symbolize the unfathomable Mystery of G^d.

Bibliography
Brown, R.M. 1984. *Unexpected News: Reading the Bible With Third World Eyes.* Phila, PA: The Westminster Press.
Crosby, M.H. 1992. *Spirituality of the Beatitudes: Matthew's Challenges For First World Christians.* Maryknoll, NY: Orbis Books.
De Garcia, A. and G. Johnson. 1986. *Evangelism and the Poor: A Biblical Challenge For the Church.* MINN: The Augsburg Publishing House.
Harrison, B.W. 1985. *Making the Connections: Essays in Feminist Social Ethics.* Boston: Beacon Press.
Johnson, E. 1992. *She Who Is: The Mystery of God in Feminist Theological Discourse.* (Tenth Anniversary Edition, 2002). New York: the Crossroad Publishing Company.
Lee, J.A.B. 2001. *The Empowerment Approach To Social Work Practice: Building The Beloved Community.* NY: Columbia University Press.
Miller, R.J., 1994. *The Complete Gospels, Scholars Translation.* Sonoma, CA: Polebridge Press.

Ross, S.A. 1998. *Extravagant Affections: A Feminist Sacramental Theology.* NY: Continuum.

Ordained a priest: 2008, Boston

COMING HOME

Eleonora Marinaro

I GREW UP IN BROOKLYN, New York, where I attended St. Rose of Lima Parish School There, the Sisters of Saint Joseph instructed me in religion but also introduced me to the lives of the saints and all things supernatural and holy. Early on, I found myself praying for others. My earliest memory of this is of being on a trolley car. My feet did not touch the floor from my seat, but I found myself praying for the other passengers. I later came to call this prayer "the prayer of the eyes," a prayer that was sent up for each person I looked at.

After I received my first Holy Communion, I tried to attend daily Mass. I needed to be as close as possible to Jesus. At lunchtime, I would keep Jesus company in the empty "downstairs" church. I knew the Mass by heart in Latin and English. I anticipated all the actions of the priest. I somehow knew, too, that I should be on "his" side of the altar rail. By eighth grade, I knew I had to do something about this call.

I tried to go to the novitiate high school to become a Sister of St. Joseph, but my mother refused me permission. I was sent to a public high school and my call to ministry was submerged. I attended college, married and had children, always holding in mind the presence of Jesus in the Eucharist.

At a very difficult time in my life, I was spontaneously "baptized in the Holy Spirit." Many other spiritual experiences followed. I began spiritual direction with Sister Kathleen, who helped me sort through my experiences. One of the areas we discerned was my intense interest in healing, psychology and spirituality.

I attended workshops in healing with Dennis and Mathew Linn , who were brothers and Jesuits. The use of the sacraments as vehicles of healing and grace became a certainty to me. I wanted to follow their example as best I could even though I was not a priest. I began having powerful dreams of being a priest while I was in Jungian analysis. I attended Iona College's Pastoral Counseling Masters Degree program. This interfaced with a Certificate Program in Spiritual Direction.

It was at this time that I learned about the women mystics, Hildegard, Julian, Therese and the Beguines, as well as the "The Illuminative Way" as a spiritual path. I was encouraged by their bravery in the face of the dictums of the institutional church – they followed their conscience.

In 1992, I found an independent Catholic group of Old Catholics in the Orthodox Catholic Church, and after a two-year training program, my husband and I were both ordained. It was a difficult step to take because we were now out of the fold of the Roman church. It was like leaving home.

At this same time, I received a Doctor of Ministry degree. We rented a small Episcopal church in Springfield, Massachusetts, and began to have weekly Mass and healing services. Many women came just to "see" a woman priest. They celebrated with me and we all cried together for the injustice.

Within the small community of Old Catholics there were not many women, and we were isolated from each other with no support systems. In 1997, we became members of the Federation of Christian Ministries, where we became vice presidents. We were thus able to support many in their desire to minister.

I continued my ministry of healing through my counseling practice and the sacraments. Jungian dream interpretation, psychotherapy and the Illuminative Way became the subjects of my PhD dissertation, and I received my Doctorate in May of 2008.

I was incorporated into Roman Catholic Womenpriests in July of 2007. I "came home," but home was not the same, and it was not ready to have me in the Roman church. I had already stepped out *contra legem* in 1992, but I gained more than I lost by having had all the intervening time to minister to others and to grow myself.

My husband David and I have co-pastored three communities over the years. We are presently serving "Turning Point Independent Catholic Community" and "Holy Angels Catholic Community." We take turns being the main presider and the homilist. We always include a healing service.

Often women will come to the Mass just to see a woman actually celebrating the Eucharist. On many of these occasions we all wind up crying, some for the loss of opportunity be a woman priest and some for the joy of finally see a woman priest celebrate. At this point, the actuality of my Roman Catholic priesthood is mind-boggling.

In general, we celebrate all of the sacraments, but reconciliation with the Roman Catholic Church after years of estrangement is a prime feature of our ministry. We share all with each other and with our congregants, and some times are comical as a tag team. We are grateful to God/de for these opportunities and look forward to continued growth.

Ordained a priest: 2007 New York

HOLY PEOPLE, HOLY MUSIC, HOLY HOUSE CHURCH

A Roman Catholic Womanpriest's Story
Bridget Mary Meehan

A S AN IRISH-AMERICAN Catholic, my faith is in my DNA. I was born in Ireland in 1948 into a warm, loving Irish family. We lived in a little gray cottage across from the Erkina River in County Laois My mother, Bridie, had mountain-moving faith and is now cheering me on from heaven. My 83 year-old dad, Jack, who is a professional musician, is alive and well, and plays a variety of sacred music on his trumpet and sax for our worship, including "holy jazz" such as *When the Saints Go Marchin' In*. My brothers, Patrick and Sean, and their families, are supportive of my calling. Ours has always been a praying family. In Ireland, we gathered around the turf fire each evening to recite the rosary. I had a sense early on that heaven and earth were closely connected, and the saints and angels, the Blessed Mother and Jesus were always nearby. I fell in love with God at a young age, and felt a deep sense of God calling me to devote my life to the Gospel.

In 1956, our family emigrated from Ireland to the United States. We attended Catholic schools in Northern Virginia. I frequently attended daily Mass in grade school, and there experienced a special closeness to Christ in the Eucharist. The call to priesthood, I believe, was imbedded in my soul in those early years of my life. After graduation from Bishop O'Connell High School, I entered the Immaculate Heart of Mary Sisters. Ten years later I took a leave of absence, and subsequently joined the Sisters for Christian Community. Through the years, I became aware that other denominations were ordaining women and I pledged myself to work for ordination of women in the Roman Catholic Church. I strongly sensed God's call to priesthood when I worked for fifteen years as a pastoral associate at Ft. Myer Chapel in Arlington, Virginia. My call to priestly ministry was confirmed by that wonderful community that I dearly loved, and by several communities that I have served over the past twelve years. One of those communities, in Northern Virginia, has met these entire twelve years to reflect on the Sunday Scripture readings in preparation for liturgy.

Since my ordination as a priest in 2006, Dad and I celebrate Eucharist in our "house church." Currently we split our time between Virginia and Florida, and are delighted to have house churches in both places.

Here is an illustration of our celebration in Sarasota. Our parishioners gather, carrying delicious foods for the meal and greeting one another. Dick and Pat lay down the warm trays of hot corned beef and cabbage on the counter and join the circle. Dad starts playing *Amazing Grace* on the sax, with a wee bit of jazz that draws all of us into the spirit of praise for our Saturday evening Mass at Mary, Mother of Jesus House Church. Our fledging community joins in the singing, opens their hearts to one another with stories of their faith lives during the shared homily, and recites the Eucharistic prayers together. "Do this in memory of me," we pray, and so we are taking Jesus' words literally and celebrating together the mysteries of our faith at the sacred banquet. All are welcome at this table of plenty. Each Eucharist is laden with grace and an opportunity to encounter extravagant, divine love. God is very fond of us, and calls us to live our lives as bread broken and wine poured, in service of our sisters and brothers. As devout Roman Catholics have done through the ages, we, the Body of Christ, are proclaiming the mysteries of our faith. The only difference is that I am a Roman Catholic womanpriest presiding in a Church that has yet to accept women's ordination. This does not bother our energized community. As one woman noted, "The Vatican will catch up one of these days." Until then, we say, "Let us praise God, you holy people, with holy music." And so we do – every week in the winter in our cozy home only a few miles from the Gulf of Mexico, and with our two communities in Northern Virginia during the summer months.

Helen Duffy, a member of our house church, said that maybe we should "pull" our ad from the local paper. She had a bad dream that the papal nuncio would come through our doors – and this would not be a good thing! I chuckled to myself. Her husband Jack has reminded us on numerous occasions that he has "had it" with Our Lady of Perpetual Responsibility and Guilt, and he is delighted to praise God at our Mary, Mother of Jesus Church. He does not share his wife's bad dream that the punitive arm of the hierarchy can hurt us.

When we put the announcement in our local paper, *The Sarasota Herald Tribune*, the Venice diocese issued an internal memo to its priests that Mary, Mother of Jesus Catholic House Church was not recognized in the diocese. Additionally, an editor from the paper informed me that a diocesan official had asked that our ad be pulled. But the *Herald Tribune* did not cave in to diocesan pressure. Score one for freedom of the press and RCWP! We are grateful that many members of our house church first became aware of us through this newspaper.

After a wonderful round of sharing, and affirmation of RCWP as a pioneering movement in the Church, our community agreed that we were indeed called to announce to our local Sarasota community that an inclusive Catholic Mass was a reality in the area and that all were welcome. As Helen was leaving, she agreed that we have nothing to fear from the hierarchy. Jesus has spoken to our hearts, and we will "rise and not be afraid" as we open our doors and our hearts to all who seek a spiritual home in our area. No one will be turned away, not even the papal nuncio!

Before going to Florida last year, Dad and I met with the PAX community, an established Northern Virginia Roman Catholic community who have hired their own priests for thirty years and planned the liturgies with these presiders. They asked me to preside at the Thanksgiving liturgy because they believed that they were "ready" for a woman priest. A liturgy team met with me for two hours to prepare this liturgy. I wore a stole at their request, and we celebrated the liturgy in a large room in a member's home. People sang joyously, shared openly, and participated fully. A festive potluck meal followed the liturgy. In both communities, in Virginia and in Sarasota, we meet on a regular basis to celebrate Eucharist.

In preparation for ordination, I earned a master's degree from The Catholic University of America, a Doctor of Ministry degree from Virginia Episcopal Seminary, and spent fifteen years in pastoral ministry. I wrote 18 books, including *Praying with Women of the Bible* and *Praying with Visionary Women*. I am the producer of GodTalkTV, a cable access television program. I am dean of the Doctor of Ministry program for Global Ministries University, an online theological program that I helped design. As a pastoral associate, I accompanied people on their spiritual journey, directed a pre-marital preparation program, conducted Communion services outside of Mass, coordinated RCIA, conducted home visitation of the sick, and ran a family-based religious education program. On more than one occasion, I felt that the Spirit was calling me to priesthood through the people in the community with whom I served.

After leaving parish ministry, I continued to serve as a leader of three small faith communities that met in my homes in both Virginia, for ten years, and Florida, for four years. On one occasion, members of our women's community in Florida called me forth to be their priest. When they had discovered that I had been invited to attend the ordinations on the St. Lawrence Seaway, the first ordinations of Roman Catholic Womenpriests in North America, the women's response was, "This is great, but we want you to be our priest!"

The word "church," *ekklesia* in the Greek, is more properly translated as "assembly." It is a gathering of persons into a spiritual community. Our fledging community not only breaks open the Word, participates in a dialogue homily, and recites the Eucharistic prayer, but also decides on whether I wear liturgical vestments. On some occasions, I have worn an alb and stole. When I presided at a large public liturgy at Call to Action, I wore an alb, stole, and chasuble. It is my custom to let the community decide how they want "their priest" to dress. (Imagine parishioners telling their pastor what to wear! Would we have a "wardrobe" dilemma?)

One woman, Marie, who had been divorced and remarried, cried when she received communion at our house church last spring. After a hostile encounter with a priest years ago, she felt unworthy to receive the Eucharist in her parish community. Now she says, "I feel like I have come home at last." Marie has invited me to celebrate Mass in her home in Florida. I plan to do home Masses when people ask. When people are sick and infirm, I gather with their family and friends in their own surroundings, to administer the sacrament of the anointing of the sick in a communal setting, inviting others to also anoint the patient, and to pray together for healing and wholeness.

A word I have heard a lot this year is "hope." Roman Catholic Womenpriests (RCWP) give Catholics renewed hope, especially alienated, marginalized Catholics like Margaret, who said: "As a young adult, I disassociated myself from the Catholic Church. I could not deal with the male dominated hierarchy. Coming to Oakwood Manor, I met Bridget. Through her and her house services, I have awakened and embraced my spirituality. I have reconnected with the Spirit of God."

Likewise, we offer hope that a renewed Church is possible for Catholics who attend weekly liturgy. Judy Beaumont, who is a practicing Catholic, expressed enthusiastic support after attendance at one of our house church liturgies: "The Church is so blessed by the priestly ministry of Bridget Mary and her sister women priests. Jesus is present through and in her, and the ordination of women brings such joy and hope for all God's people. I feel that God has graced us and revealed new ways of thinking and being Church through the Womenpriest movement."

This hopefulness became evident when a group of our Irish friends, who generally "pay, pray and obey" in their local parishes each week, invited me to bless a new home and celebrate a Sunday liturgy there. Using holy water from Mary's Shrine in Knock, Ireland, all of us walked through the house, blessing each room as we processed. Usually, our Irish friends do not volunteer to read in church. They felt comfortable in our house church; they read, shared in the dialogue homily, and prayed the words of consecration together with me. When all was finished, they pronounced the liturgy "brilliant!" They noted that it was a big step forward from their worship experience at Sunday liturgy in the local parish, and one in which Ireland's patron saint, Brigit, Bishop of Kildare, would have felt right at home – blessing everything with water to remind us of God's protective presence! (St. Brigit's cross hangs over the door of many Irish homes and barns as a sign of protection and blessing.)

Roman Catholic womenpriests are dreaming daring dreams and discovering fresh visions. Jack Duffy, one of our Sarasota house church members, shares what it means to worship in spirit and truth as the Body of Christ: "In this small, intimate, friendly, around-the-table setting, the worship was deep, spiritual, holy. We could all really sense that Jesus was there with us. This is the way early Christians celebrated the Lord's Supper, during the time of the Acts of the Apostles, and for the first 200 to 300 years, before we became encumbered with big buildings."

Yes, indeed, we have come full circle. Like our sisters and brothers in the early Christian community, we bless and share the sacred meal in Mary, Mother of Jesus House Church. We believe that Christ is calling us to go forth, filled with God's love and compassion, to minister as partners and equals with all God's people. The world is our parish. As my Southern neighbors say, "Y'all come!"

I believe that Christ is calling us to step out of the boat and walk on water. Acting *contra legem* is the only way forward. We must break the law in order to change the law. An unjust law as St. Augustine said, is no law at all. We have an obligation to disobey an unjust law. We are practicing "holy disobedience" to a law that discriminates against women in the Church, a law that contradicts our equality as baptized members of the Church. In Gal: 3:28, we read: "In Christ, there is no Jew, or Greek, slave or citizen, male or female, all are one in Christ Jesus." As Cardinal Walter Kasper, who heads the Vatican Pontifical Commission for Christian Unity, said, "Some situations oblige us to obey God and one's own conscience, rather than the leaders of the Church. Indeed, one may even be obliged to accept excommunication, rather than act against one's conscience." St. Thomas Aquinas once said, "I would rather die excommunicated than to have violated my conscience."

Excommunication cannot nullify one's baptism. It is important to know that excommunication, whether automatic excommunication or formal excommunication, cannot put a person out of the Church. In recent years, politicians who are pro-choice have incurred this penalty in some dioceses. Divorced and remarried Catholics who did not receive an annulment also incur automatic excommunication. However, once one is baptized into the Catholic community, one is always Catholic.

There are a number of holy women, role models in the Church, who practiced holy disobedience to hierarchical oppression. One such role model was St. Joan of Arc. When Joan was asked whether she was subject to Church authorities, she replied, "Yes, but our Lord must be served first." In the eighteenth century, Mother Theodore Guerin, the founder of the Sisters of Providence, was threatened with excommunication. In October 2006, Pope Benedict presided at her canonization. In one century the Church censures and excommunicates, in the next century, the Church canonizes.

It is my hope that one day the Church that I love will recognize Roman Catholic womenpriests as holy women and men who have led the Church into a renewed model of priestly ministry, rooted in the vision of Jesus, who called women and men to be disciples and equals. The call for the full equality of women in the Church is the voice of God in our time. Perhaps a future pope (dare I say a womanpriest?) will affirm our courageous example of Gospel equality as a gift to the people of God. In the meantime, I will celebrate the extravagant love of the Christ-presence in Eucharistic liturgies with holy music in holy house churches wherever I am!

Ordained a priest: 2006, Pittsburgh

BLESSED ARE THE PEACEMAKERS

Janice Sevre-Duszynska

M Y MOTHER'S PARENTS CAME from Poland and we lived in my Busia's (grandmother's) house, so from an early age I became aware of places other than the U.S. and also of the horrors of war. At least once a month, my Busia received a letter from her family in Waclowek. When it came, my mother would stop whatever she was doing and answer it, in Polish, and I would mail the response – all within just a few hours. My Busia never saw her twin sister again after she left Poland in 1910.

I heard stories, from my mother and my aunts, of my Busia worrying about her family during and after World War II. They said she sent money to an agency in New York that worked with an agency in Germany to get hams, sugar, flour and butter to her relatives, as well as money for heat during the cold Polish winters. As a nine year-old girl in 1959, I watched the documentary on TV with my mother about the occupation of Poland and the concentration camps. The effects of hearing those stories and seeing those photos have never left me.

Nor have the stories about my uncles and the neighbor men who fought during the war. I saw the shrapnel on the cheek and leg of Georgie, the grocery man at Banicki's neighborhood store. My mother told me the stories of her three brothers in the war. Uncle Steve, for example, could barely turn his head as a result of the arthritis he acquired in the trenches.

Our Uncle Hank haunted the house with his memories of the Battle of the Bulge. "Janice," he said to me one Sunday afternoon when I was about ten, "your Busia and Dzia Dzia taught us to be peace-loving. The sisters and priests at St. Cyril's taught us it was a sin to kill. Yet, during the war I killed other human beings." There was no end to his trauma, and each of us children, my cousins, and our family recognized in his suffering the lasting effects of chaos.

Later in life, when I began teaching English as a Second Language to high school students from all over the world, many of whom were refugees from war-torn countries, I knew that eventually I would have to make a statement for peace in behalf of those children and what they had endured. That was when I decided to cross the line at Ft. Benning (Georgia) on November 15, 2001, in a peaceful demonstration to close the School of the Americas.

My three months in federal prison were a transformative experience. I realized that I could endure the dehumanization that characterizes prison life. I also learned that I could be of use to the women there. During the first six weeks of prison life, I observed and listened to what the women taught me. After the second six weeks, as I taught them reading and writing, many of the women began confessing to me, sharing their stories and their tears, telling of how they had gotten here and asking for forgiveness.

One woman in our small room of eight to ten women told me something that shook the very ground of my being. "I know that the God inside of you is real," she cried to me, her tears wetting me. That was a sign to me from Holy Wisdom that I could work for peace and endure the consequences. I am happiest when I am on the streets, or on military bases or nuclear test sites, or in deserts witnessing for peace and justice and the Kin-dom.

My ministry for peace and justice grew alongside my witnessing for women's ordination. As a young girl, I had wanted to be an altar girl. I cleaned the sacristy and the sanctuary every Saturday morning with Sister de Paul for six or seven years. When I was alone in the church, I imagined myself celebrating Mass. I read the Gospel and preached. I made believe I held up the Eucharist and shared it. I blessed the people of God. I felt as natural on the altar as I did in our backyard. I felt no fear.

One Saturday morning when I was about ten, I felt inspired. When the altar boys rang the bell for Mass, I was ready to follow the priest into the sanctuary, which was "off limits" to me unless I was dead and in a coffin, or a bride. I was aware of these inequities based on gender. The altar boy rang the bell and I followed behind the priest, determined to cross over into the sacred space of the sanctuary. I heard a gasp, and turned. There was Sister de Paul, understanding what I was about to do. The fearful look on her face told me that she would be punished for my actions. I knew that moment that someday I would return to the sanctuary.

Years later, on January 17, 1998, my forty-eighth birthday, I asked Bishop Kendrick Williams of Lexington, Kentucky, to ordain me during an ordination at the Cathedral of Christ the King. While he did not do so, the Spirit inspired me to witness to the U.S. bishops at their biannual meetings in November in Washington, D.C., and in the summer in various cities across the country.

From witnessing to the bishops, I learned to write liturgies for the various reform groups that would gather in front of the hotels or the cathedrals where the bishops met. As time went by, I learned to give the service to the people and to serve more as a facilitator as we prayed and sang. In my work as Minister of Irritation for the Women's Ordination Conference, I have been blessed to meet many Spirited men and women who have walked the road with me and inspired me, for which I am grateful. Their sharing continues to be grace-filled.

All of my experiences and the people alongside them – mother, wife, sister, aunt, divorced woman, step-grandmother, teacher, a parent who has lost a child, a former prisoner of conscience, my work as an activist – all are the "teachers" that have helped shape me in preparation for ministry. My studies for a Master's in theology and my present work in a Doctor of Ministry program have enabled me to come full circle in preparation for the servant priesthood.

Much of my peace and justice work is within the interfaith community, and from these people I have been affirmed. Over the years, they have recognized my desire for priesthood and they have encouraged me in every way.

The world cries out to hear the Gospels interpreted from women's lived experiences. The world cries out for feminine images of God and women on the altar. With the gifts that the Spirit continues to give, Jesus the Nonviolent One calls us to work for the Kin-dom and its gracious, generous, compassionate God of abundance. As children of God, we are not to follow unjust laws.

Ordained a priest: 2008, Lexington

Joan Houk, Priest
Rose Marie (Ree) Dunn Hudson, Priest
Elsie Hainz McGrath, Priest
Mary Ellen Robertson, Priest
Kathy Sullivan Vandenberg, Priest

Great Waters priests Cheryl Bristol, Kathy Vandenberg, Joan Houk, Elsie McGrath, Rose Marie Hudson, Mary Ellen Robertson, Judith McKloskey at Therese of Divine Peace in St. Louis.

At ordination in St Louis: Kathy Redig, guest priest, Bridget Mary Meehan, Rose Marie Hudson, Patricia Fresen, Jean Marchant, Elsie McGrath, Judith McKloskey, guest bishop, Janice Sevre-Duszynska.

JOURNEYING STEP BY STEP

Joan Houk

J OURNEYS TAKE DIFFERENT FORMS. A woman boards an airplane at JFK Airport in New York and touches down on the tarmac in Los Angeles within hours. Or with road map in hand, she can slide into the driver's seat of her car, cruise the interstate highways, stay overnights in motels, and arrive in California in a few days. If she wishes to listen to the prompting of the Spirit in the voices and lives of those near her, she may choose to make the trip on foot. Step by step, with no detailed map, she moves on her journey, guided by those around her and her internal compass. This last is the form my journey has taken.

My journey to ordination in the Roman Catholic priesthood has been a "step by step" process. Baptized as an infant and educated in Catholic schools for twelve years by the Sisters of Mercy, I was well formed and informed in my faith. I received the sacraments of baptism, reconciliation, Eucharist, confirmation and marriage in St. Francis Xavier Church. Church was my second family, and parish my second home.

As my husband's career took us to several states, the first thing I always did upon arrival in our new location was to register in the Catholic parish. Even before all the boxes were unpacked, I was actively participating in parish events and adult programs. As my children grew, I became involved "step by step" in catechesis, followed by youth ministry, social outreach, and then leading prayer services. I was called forth by pastors and community members, first by Catholic parishioners, and later by peers from other Christian Churches. During those years, I continued my education. I received a B.A. in Elementary Education from St. Martin's College, and had begun a masters program in religious education when a new baby and relocation from the West to East Coast caused a detour in my plans. "Step by step," I followed my internal compass – the Holy Spirit deep in my heart.

The threat of nuclear warfare hung over our world from the 1970's into the 80's. My advocacy in the peace movement led me to graduate study and an M.S. in Conflict Management from George Mason University. Little did I realize that this field of study and the skills involved in resolving conflict would become most valuable to me in my future work in the Church. "Step by step," the Spirit led me to where I needed to go.

Upon listening to the Spirit, and to clergy members and those in the laity, over time it finally became clear to me that I was being called to priesthood in my Roman Catholic Church. I set out to prepare for ordination by applying to the Master of Divinity Program at the University of Notre Dame. I was accepted into the seminary program, where my fieldwork included one year in each of these areas: marriage preparation of ecumenical and interfaith couples, marriage annulment cases, and hospital chaplaincy. I received my M.Div. degree from Notre Dame in 1996. What was the next "step" going to be?

The Spirit stirred in me. She spoke to me through diverse people. In the end, She planted my feet firmly upon Appalachian soil deep in the hills and "hollers" of Kentucky. I was hired by the Diocese of Lexington and installed by Bishop Kendrick Williams as Pastoral Director of Holy Cross Church, a parish without a resident pastor. My family and I lived in the building that served as worship site, office, parish hall, outreach center, and home. I was happy to serve the people, those few who were Catholic and the many who were not. The local ministerial association welcomed me as the new Catholic "pastor" and invited me to join them in ecumenical collaboration. While I was leading and ministering, I was patiently waiting until the day the Church would ordain me.

In the spring of 2000, I was encouraged by diocesan leadership to become the Pastoral Director of St. Patrick Church, a Church established in 1867, which was going to be without a resident pastor for the first time. All of my past experience, education and skills came together as I ministered pastorally to the parishioners. My ministry was spiritually rewarding, and yet there was a sadness as well. I prayed with those who were sick and dying, but could not anoint with oil. I listened to troubled people, but could not give absolution. When a priest could not be with us on Sunday morning, I could lead a Liturgy of the Word and distribute communion, but could not consecrate the Eucharist. I was well prepared to be their priest, but I was a woman. The Spirit called, the people called, the hierarchy said, "No."

It became more and more difficult to remain patient as I waited for ordination to open up to me. The Spirit was troubled. The people had needs, and the hierarchy was turning its back. The Spirit sent vocations, but the hierarchy refused to listen. My heart became heavy. "Step by step," my journey continued.

A postcard arrived in the mail: a conference to be held in Philadelphia. The Spirit whispered, "You can visit your sister nearby. Come to the conference." So I did. My husband John and I listened as Patricia Fresen spoke of unjust laws, and of how sometimes we must break the law in order to change it. She had broken civil law in South Africa because it discriminated against Blacks and Coloreds. South African people broke the apartheid laws, and apartheid was brought to an end. The Church was guilty of the sin of discrimination against women and blaming God for it, and indeed, continues to do so to this day. Canon 1024, which says, "A baptized male alone receives sacred ordination validly," is an unjust law. As Patricia Fresen spoke of prophetic obedience, the Spirit was speaking to John and me. That day, we knew what I had to do. I would obey God and break an unjust law.

On July 31, 2006, I was ordained a Roman Catholic Womanpriest, *contra legem* – against the law – by Bishops Patricia Fresen, Gisela Forster and Ida Raming. Since my ordination, I have anointed, absolved and consecrated. The people request my ministry, and I am blessed and anointed by God to serve them. I am Catholic, and I stay connected to the Roman Catholic Church through my membership in my geographical, diocesan parish even though I am not permitted to minister by the Church hierarchy. I look forward to the day when the Church officially recognizes the ordination of women. I believe that it will happen.

So my journey continues "step by step." What is the next step? Only the Spirit knows. I wait and listen.

Ordained a priest: 2006, Pittsburgh

I THINK I SEE A PRIEST

Rose Marie (Ree) Dunn Hudson

I THINK I SEE A priest. I do see a priest!"
These were the words of Rabbi Susan Talve following the greatest moment of my life: my priestly ordination. Our eyes met and we knew that something special had just happened: a Jewish rabbi and a Roman Catholic priest celebrating a moment in history that most people of our generation thought they would never see. There were those who said that the event would harm Jewish-Catholic relations, but just the opposite happened. Having a Catholic ordination in a Jewish synagogue opened the way for renewed dialogue and the possibility for stronger personal and community relationships. We are already involved in intrareligious groups in St. Louis, Missouri and elsewhere.

As I reflect on my path to priesthood, flashbacks of my childhood come to mind. I was born in Flat River, Missouri; a lead-mining town located in St. Francois County. The entire county was known at the time as the lead-mining capitol of the world. My parents lived in an old, ugly brown-sided house behind the local Disciples of Christ church. I was born in that house. Those were the days when doctors came to the homes for birthing and medical treatment. Prior to my birth, Daddy said my name would be Rose Marie. Those were the days before people knew what the gender of a baby would be. I always thought that made me special. He seemed to know I would be a girl. The rest of my siblings were boys.

Most of the men in Flat River worked in the lead mines. Fortunately, Daddy did not. We did not have to see him come home with lead dust all over him. There were accidents in the mines. They were not discussed much. It went with the territory. I often wondered how it looked underground, but I soon learned I would never know because of my gender. The men would not allow women underground because they considered it bad luck.

Almost all the men in town liked to fish and hunt. The couple across the street went fishing nearly every weekend. They would come over to our home and play cards with my parents. I loved to hear adults talk, so I would often eavesdrop on their conversation. After being on a fishing trip, the couple would argue about who caught the largest fish. In their case it was usually the woman. I remember thinking how neat it was, that women could do more than cook, clean, and raise children.

I attended Eugene Field Elementary School, which was at the end of the street we lived on. I loved going to school, especially recess, when we would play softball. Most of the girls would go off and play with dolls, swing, jump rope and talk. This was boring to me. I wondered why boys could have so much fun and girls had to sit around. I played with the boys all the time, and I out-played all of them. They got to compete against the other elementary schools in the community. When it became time to compete, the boys wanted me to be on the team, but I could not be on the team because of being a girl.

Repeatedly, as time went by, I learned what a disadvantage it was to be a girl. A woman's role in society was pretty much culturally determined. Men or boys always had the lead positions, except in areas they considered feminine: secretary, teacher or nurse. I held the job of President of the Future Teachers of America Club, most of whom were girls. I was also in the lead positions in my church youth groups, which most of the boys did not care about. It was through my Methodist church that I received a lot of nurturing from many caring adults. They recognized my gifts and encouraged me. Many of them said I was a born leader and a born teacher. This was prophetic in that I was a teacher for forty years, and I had many leadership roles in the teaching profession.

I remember feeling comfortable and accepted by my Methodist church community. I was exactly where I needed to be. I attended church camp every season from the time I was twelve. The church supported youth who wanted to attend. The third year I attended, I was fourteen and already deeply involved in the MYF (Methodist Youth Fellowship). It was during this year, at an evening campfire service, that I clearly became aware of my call to vocation in the church. Exodus 3:7 says, "I have heard the groans of my people." My prophetic vocation began with a call from God. It continued with listening to the groans of the community and giving them a voice. The voice of my Methodist community was very supportive, especially a women's group called WSCS (Women's Society Christian Service). They surrounded me with their love. Opportunities for experience and service were made available. Prophetic obedience, with strong possibilities of faith, was an ever-present reality at that time of my life. Later, the WSCS financed my education through a full grant to study at

Scarritt College for Christian Workers in Nashville, Tennessee. I earned my first theological degree at Scarritt, and served for three years as a home missionary at mission schools in Georgia and New Mexico.

After serving in mission schools for the Methodist Church, I turned my attention to a correctional facility in Indiana. It seemed that periodically service to those in prison was a call in my life. While attending college, I spent a summer working for the Vermont Council of Churches. My last assignment there had been three weeks in a girl/boy correctional facility. A friend had alerted me to this job.

That same friend called me to the Indiana State Girl's School. While teaching there, I met Bob Hudson, who eventually became my husband. Prior to our marriage, I told him that I had been called to serve God and God's holy people, that I was moving toward the ordained ministry and sometime in the future it would happen. I said if he wanted to marry me under those circumstances, I would marry him. He looked at me rather skeptically and said yes. In April 2006, four children and eleven grandchildren later, I sat with my husband and said, "The time has come. I'm going to become a priest." He calmly replied, "You said it would happen during our conversation in 1966."

Priesthood wasn't in my mind then, but becoming a Methodist preacher was. As time passed, the prompting of the Holy Spirit continued to fill me with a sense of urgency to pursue my calling. Ordination of women in the Methodist Church was beginning. I became very excited, applied and was accepted to enter the formation program to become a Methodist preacher. I taught during the day, did family things constantly, and studied at night. When I was age 38, about one and a half months before I was to be ordained a Methodist minister, my husband and I went on a retreat called Marriage Encounter, which focused on communication and spirituality. On the way home, my husband said, "Honey, I want to be a Catholic."

I could not believe he was saying this, although this Catholic-based weekend had been one of the most positive events in our married life. Our children were attending Catholic school at the time and were also interested in becoming Catholics. In the final analysis, this is something all of them wanted to do.

With the entire family leaning towards Catholicism, I knew I had to make this decision alone. I contacted a Benedictine monastery I had visited many years before, and asked if I could spend a few days there. They asked no questions, and said I could come. And after three days, I felt the Spirit say, "You've been a Protestant for 38 years. Now you will become a Catholic and see what that faith community is like. Later you'll be a catalyst to help bring the whole church back together again." For me, that was the complete answer. In 1978 my whole family joined the Catholic Church.

I've been involved in everything a woman could do in the Catholic Church, I helped educate children in the faith and I helped with liturgies. But I was always nagged, always hounded by this feeling that I should be doing something more. When I got to be 60, I said, "You know, God, I'm not getting any younger."

In 2006, I had the privilege of meeting Bishop Patricia Fresen, who had been ordained a Roman Catholic bishop in 2005. She spoke about her experiences. Before she led the Eucharistic celebration, she said, "If there's anyone here who is called to ordained ministry, please come forward."

I went forward. I was accepted into the discernment process in May of 2006. During the year of discernment, I spent a year studying the sacraments, which I had done a few years before with the St. Louis Archdiocesan Office of Laity and Family Life. It was a good update. While this process was going on, it was my privilege to attend the first womenpriest's ordinations in the United States, in Pittsburgh, Pennsylvania. Women came from all over the United States. Others came from Europe and other parts of the planet. I had never been so excited. We left on the ship and the ceremony began as we floated the waters of the Ohio, the Monongahela, and the Allegheny, the famous three rivers. Joy and unity were the words of the day for me. It was the beginning of a difficult journey, but one my colleague and I looked forward to with great anticipation. In November 2006, I attended another meeting where all of the newly ordained womenpriests celebrated a public Mass for a standing-room-only congregation. Patricia Fresen had asked if we would be ready for diaconal ordination on August 11, 2007 in Minneapolis. I had said, "Yes," but my colleague had not. Following the Mass, a friend captured the moment on camera when my friend said, "Yes." We prepared, and on August 11, 2007 we went to Minneapolis.

As I lie on the floor, prostrate before my God, I felt a heaviness on my back. When I tried to get up, I couldn't. Someone helped me up. The haunting singing of *Veni Sancte Spiritus* was flowing over me and I unconsciously began to sing. Later, my colleague said she heard me singing and a friend said he noticed my inability to rise from the floor. He said it was the Holy Spirit – that the same thing happened when he was ordained a priest. What a tremendous confirmation of ordination, I thought.

Following the ceremony there was a receiving line. From that experience came forth three phrases that live with me today.

Repeatedly people said, "Your courage gives me hope." Others said, "You go girl!" One very young woman said, "The force be with you." She looked again into my eyes and said, "The force is with you." At that moment, I knew I was God's woman priest forever. Before leaving Minneapolis Bishop Patricia said she would be in contact soon regarding priestly ordination. Within a week of returning home, Patricia said she would be return to the United States for a meeting in November and would like to ordain my colleague and I a week later. I cannot write this part of my story as "I" because "We" were involved in everything together from that time forward, along with many friends and family members.

Rabbi Susan Talve said, "Yes!"

Her board said, "Yes."

The people said, "Yes."

Elsie McGrath and I said, "Yes!"

We knew the event would be huge – but not to the extent that it became. A reformist Jewish congregation was about to allow their space for a Roman Catholic Womanpriest ordination, a movement seen as schismatic to the Roman Catholic hierarchical church. Everybody was saying "yes" except for the hierarchal church, which was and remains unable to say yes, not for the reasons they speak but for fear of relinquishing their position of power and authority.

Susan Talve stood fast, refusing to be intimidated by threatening letters and people sent in to talk to her and strongly discourage her hosting in such an event. I personally received five written communications from the archbishop, as did my colleague. Often late at night a "process server" would come and serve me with another document or decree. These were all attempts at intimidation, trying to frighten us into submission.

I, along with my colleague, sent the archbishop a letter of our intentions on October 1, 2007. The week following the letter, we were asked to come and meet at the Archdiocesan Offices with what turned out to be a canon lawyer. He asked questions about the RCWP movement and about our personal lives. We left and decided not to return. On November 5, 2007, we each received a letter of canonical admonition threatening excommunication; on November 11, 2007; a decree of contumacy and forfeiture of the exercise of the right of defense; and on March 12, 2008, a Declaration of Excommunication. This is a hurtful and despicable process that ascends from the Middle Ages and has no bearing on anything.

Excommunication is only a word, and I have not accepted this label put on me by the Catholic hierarchy I have followed my prophetic call to priesthood; one that was fulfilled 54 years after the original prompting of the Holy Spirit on that special evening at church camp in 1953.

I had no idea that just wanting to serve God and God's holy people would precipitate so much controversy. I am about the process of the renewal and reform of God's holy church, the people of God, and this will never change as long as I live.

Following the laying on of hands by the bishop and all of the assembled clergy, the people of God began coming. To this very day I feel their hands on me. The people of God in Minneapolis and the people of God in St. Louis ordained me to serve God, them, and all of God's church.

Yes, our eyes met, Susan Talve's and mine. I had the realization that my priesthood was a culmination of all that happened in my life, a fulfillment of renewal, of God's continued call and the continuous call of communities as I march on toward the goal of unity in the church of Jesus the Christ. A catalyst I am, and a catalyst I will continue to be. Christ was anointed, and so am I. I accept this anointing, not counting the cost, and press on toward the mark of my high calling.

Ordained a priest: 2007 St. Louis

THE ROAD LESS TRAVELED BY*

Canonical Disobedience in St. Louis
Elsie Hainz McGrath

> Two roads diverged in a wood, and I –
> *I took the one less traveled by,*
> *And that has made all the difference.*
> --Robert Frost--

I had a clear and clearly Spirit-inspired vision of ordained priesthood very late in life. I was 67-years old, retired, and in self-exile from the Church I had loved and served constantly during the previous 32 years. Life was sweet – laid-back and fairly uncomplicated. And suddenly I was applying to a program of formation for illegal ordination as a Roman Catholic priest. *What was I thinking?*

It was a question that lots of people asked me in the weeks and months that followed. I tried to formulate a coherent, logical answer – but there was none. Clearly, I *wasn't* thinking. I was simply, finally, *listening.*

In retrospect, it was all so clear, of course: the years of study, the ministry-related employments, the volunteer work for the archdiocese, and later the parish. Even my teen years, before I was a Catholic, held hints of what was to come. Why else would I have volunteered to preach a sermon to my congregation when I was 15? Or spent hours in religious discussions with a fundamentalist Christian between classes at a public high school? Or even become a Catholic at the age of 17? It seems that, from my youth, the only thing that continually held my interest *and* moved me to "push the envelope" of conventional thought was religion.

I had been married and become a Catholic at age 17, was a mother by age 18, a grandmother at 38, a great-grandmother at 58, and was widowed at 59. During that 42-year stretch, I had volunteered for everything from Cub Scout den mother to RCIA catechist. My husband and I had a highly respected and called-upon team ministry in Catholic marriage preparation, over a period of 15 years, throughout the state of Missouri and into Illinois. I had also worked full time while earning theology degrees from Saint Louis University and the Aquinas Institute of Graduate Theology; accompanied my husband through his seminary-based program of preparation for the ordained permanent diaconate; and been an accomplished editor and writer in a Catholic publishing house.

There was no question in my mind that, left alone to do it, I could. I had the academic qualifications, the vocational background, the life experience. I knew I could be a good priest ever since my days as a supermarket checker, when I became my customers' "confessor" across the checkout counter. I recognized that, with much pain, when my late husband was ordained a permanent deacon and I was left sitting on the other side of the altar rail. Was it reason enough to pursue ordination, that certain knowledge I had that I *could* do it? Especially in light of the public exposure it would bring to me? Did this constitute a "call"?

What, I wondered, would I lose for standing firm in this undertaking? I knew it would be, by far, the most public exposure of my lifetime. I *still* strongly dislike controversy. I've *always* wanted everybody to like me. I'm not "good on my feet," when attacks and arguments are being orally waged against me. Sure, I could take it – but could I take it graciously and intelligently? Could I take it without making a mockery of the whole movement? Could I take it and advance the cause for Church renewal?

I am a quiet, self-conscious, hearing-impaired woman. I am also an out-spoken, self-assured, and courageous woman when I am faced with public moral dilemmas. I will not be cowed because there is always something more on the line than my own well-being in such situations. I am setting a precedent and an example for those who are watching, for those who are coming after. I owe it to them to not cave in to pressure and intimidation, regardless of the personal outcome. In the past, I have lost jobs and lost friends for standing firm. High price to pay, but I could not do otherwise – and every time God's providence brought something better and more beautiful into my life because of it.

My discernment on pursuing ordination, *contra legem*, led me to the realization that this was not just about me. It was, in fact, not about me *at all* It was about the Church. It was about my great-granddaughters. It was about justice, Christianity, the oneness of the universe and every living thing. It was *that huge* – and *because* I could do it, I could *not* do otherwise.

A story was once told to me of the person who complained to God about the heavy cross she had to bear. So God invited her to choose a different one. She was led into "the cross room," in which were displayed crosses of every size and weight imaginable. How could she even *begin* to find the perfect cross among so many?

The woman began making her way through the room, trying on this cross and that cross, and finding none to her liking. Some were way too heavy, others were light as feathers but didn't fit right. Some were way too big, others were minuscule but wouldn't stay in place. She was feeling desperate as the day waned and she still had not found the cross for her.

Then she spotted one standing off to the side, very near the door. Why hadn't she noticed it before? She went over and tried it on – and it was perfect! Happy, she carried it out of the room and stood before God. "This one," she said, "this is the one I want."

"Of course," replied God, "it is the very one you carried in here this morning."

I follow this road in wonder and awe, and with great joy. But it is a huge onus – the cross that I must take up daily because it is *my* cross. Jesus told us that the burden was light, and therein lay the paradox, because it *is* truly a burden but truly light. And every time another person says to me, "Thank you for doing this, thank you for your courage," I am reminded of Winston Churchill's famous words [paraphrased]: "Never have so many depended upon so few for so much."

I am not ordained into "another denomination" (a common question) because my ordination has nothing to do with ordination, *per se*. My ordination has to do with justice; it has to do with reform; it has to do with solidarity and freedom and world community. My personal vision is not of a woman at every altar, but of a community of equals in every gathering place of worship. My personal vision, in fact, allows the priesthood of all believers equal access to the altar.

So it is that my colleague and I co-pastor a real church community in a real church setting – currently in the chapel of a Unitarian church that is located a few short blocks away from our archbishop's magnificent Cathedral Basilica. In fact, it is located directly across the street from the synagogue that became world-famous because it opened its doors in welcoming *shalom* for our ordinations.

Unbelievably, these past few months have been kind of our "15 minutes of fame" time, as we are both readily recognized in the area because of the inordinate amount of publicity that was generated by the archbishop's extremely public opposition to our ordination in a synagogue. People want to "touch" us, commend our "courage," even procure our "autograph" for young daughters and granddaughters. *This* makes my heart beat faster because they so obviously are sharing my own hope for the future.

In a sense, the focus of our ministry was both altered and solidified by the shameful display of high-handed vitriol on the part of the Catholic Church in St. Louis. We agreed early on that we wanted to co-pastor a church, but there were obvious problems with that ideal. The most obvious, and immediate, were lack of facility and lack of money. When the archdiocese discovered that our ordinations would happen in a mid-city synagogue, pressure was immediately applied to the synagogue's rabbi and her Board members. Archbishop Burke, famous for facing down prominent Catholics (i.e., John Kerry), was ill-prepared for resistance from a "mere" Jewess and Board members who supported the idea of this socially-active and inclusive place of worship and welcome.

All the other synagogues had vacated the confines of the city years ago; Susan Talve and her congregation put down roots. When they began, they had no synagogue. Susan shared the story with us of how the fledgling group asked the Unitarians for refuge, and were warmly welcomed. They stayed for years, and then they built their own synagogue – right across the street.

And so it was that my colleague and I walked across the street and asked for a refuge wherein we could begin to form our own fledgling community. And so it was that by the time we issued our press release for the ordinations we could include specifics of a *new* inclusive community in mid-town St. Louis – this one Roman Catholic, and co-pastored by two validly-ordained women.

In honor of our patron saints, Therese of Lisieux and Teresa of Avila, and of our never-ending prayer for *shalom* and our own recent experiences of *shalom* at the hands of Jews and Unitarians, we named our church Therese of Divine Peace Inclusive Community. Then, for good measure, we added two more "namesakes" to the mix: Teresa of Calcutta and Theresa Chikaba. Here's why.

Therese of Lisieux languished in illness until what would appear to have been an untimely death at age 24. But it was at precisely age 24 that men were allowed the sacrament of ordination, and Therese was called to be a priest. She said she would rather die than be denied the joy of following her call, and so she did. On her feast day, October 1, my colleague and I wrote our letter to Archbishop Burke telling him of our intention to ordination. We pointed out to him that it was Therese's feast day and that she is the patron of women's ordination.

(His response was to have his Defender of the Bond contact us for a "conversation" at which a woman took notes of his questions and our answers. This was termed "preliminary" to a meeting that the archbishop would set up with us.)

Teresa of Avila was an outspoken critic of the sins and excesses of the Church. She was totally unafraid to speak truth to power, was subjected to canonical inquisitions much harsher than present-day ones, and ultimately succeeded in reforming religious life. On her feast day, October 15, we issued our press release, in which we noted Teresa as a patron of church reform.

(Burke's response was to have us "served" at our homes with a Canonical Admonition: two pages of "instruction" and "warning" and "pastoral solicitation." Little had we known that this would be the archbishop's idea of a "meeting.")

Teresa of Calcutta was the epitome of servant of the margins. She claimed no fame, grew old before her time, and continued to minister to God's most needy and despised population, acting completely out of her faith that this was what she was supposed to do, and that this was where Christ could most readily be found. We recognize that our own ministry is largely to the people on the margins of a Church that dishonors them because of gender or lifestyle or sexual orientation.

(Burke's response was to have us "served" at the synagogue, immediately at the conclusion of the ordination liturgy, with a Summons and Canonical Admonition to appear in court the following month. We did not respond to this "summons" because: we would have had to plead "guilty" to the charges of heresy and schism, and recant, which is of course a lie; or plead "not guilty" and prove him and/or "them" wrong, which is of course impossible. Further, had we gone, we would have been "granting" him a position of authority over us – one of the very things we want to eradicate in our new model of priestly ministry.)

Theresa Chikaba was added to our patrons immediately before our first Mass. She ties us closely to our ordaining bishop, to whom we also grant no position of authority (illustrated by our prostration only before the altar at our ordination; the bishop moves to the side). Theresa was born and reared in Africa (but West rather than South) and she became a Dominican sister (but in Spain rather than her homeland). She was actually a black African princess, but she was kidnapped by Spanish sailors and put into servitude when she was 10-years old. She was sold into a wealthy household that adopted her into the family. Wanting to be a nun, she was refused because she was black, but was "allowed" to move into the convent as a maid. Eventually, through others' experience of Theresa as intelligent and caring, she was professed.

(Isn't it so true that if we all took the time to really know one another, there would be no stigma of racism or classism or sexism, no hatred or vengeance or war? Burke's reaction to that first Mass, though, was to again "serve" us at our homes with a Decree of Contumacy and Forfeiture of the Exercise of the Right of Defense. We could now be "judged" and "punished" with no recourse – and no remorse.)

We have been happily celebrating weekly Eucharist since the First Sunday of Advent, December 2007, in the chapel of the First Unitarian Church of St. Louis, who continues to host fledgling communities looking for a place of refuge. We have been invited to share and worship with Unitarians in Kansas City, MO and in Quincy, IL through our association with our St. Louis hosts. As pastors in the mid-city area, we have also been invited into the worship-based community-and-neighborhood-building initiative that originated at the synagogue across the street – that site of the most glorious, inclusive, joy-and-faith-filled ordination celebration imaginable.

(Burke's response to our weekly liturgy was a final – maybe – serving of papers. This one, coming four months after ordination, was the Decree of Excommunication. We now had the distinction of being the only RCWP women who have been formally excommunicated since the Danube Seven.)

Nowadays, I can barely keep up with things. I have never been so busy, nor so happy. I have a special ministry to nursing home residents, am pursuing a Doctoral degree, and seem to be on something of a speaking circuit. I also mentor women who are discerning ordination, both as formation director for RCWP and as spiritual companion for WOC. All this and a wonderful parish to pastor too! As the saying on one of my tee shirts goes: *This is what a woman priest looks like!*

The ordination, at which we had originally projected an attendance of around 200, was a standing-room-only crowd of 600-plus – a microcosm of the world. The first Mass, in a 100-person capacity chapel, was a standing-room-only crowd of at least 150 – a microcosm of church. Some were curiosity-seekers, sure; but most were supporters or prodigal sons and daughters seeking refuge, a home, community.

In St. Louis, people are finding their voice. Truth is being spoken to power. Hope is being restored and church is being renewed as pilgrims from every walk of life and every sphere of religious belief are coming together. We share our common goals and create new ones. We share our common prayer and learn new ones. We share our common faith and enrich new ones. We stand on Holy Ground, hand-in-hand, and march courageously along the pilgrims' way, the road less traveled by.

*Robert Frost, *The Road Less Traveled By*

Ordained a priest: 2007, St. Louis

MY STORY

Mary Ellen Robertson

FROM AN EARLY AGE, I had a desire to help people who were in need, especially the sick, the elderly, and those in need of a listening presence. I have been in formation my whole life. Celebration of life comes in the presence of the moment, in lived experience, and in liturgical celebration of the stages of life.

Ministries of spiritual direction, pastoral care, spiritual writing, and liturgy have developed out of life experience. Many experiences of service in family life – my own as a daughter, wife, parent and grandparent; and my witness of the lived experiences of my parents, spouse, daughters and grandchildren – have taught me about the needs we all have and the importance of a prayerful presence.

While in my junior year at Providence Hospital School of Nursing, my oldest brother, Bob, was ordained a Roman Catholic priest. For his ordination, his five siblings – Dick, Tom, Fred, Sally and I – gave him his first chalice with each of our names engraved on it. Little did I know then that forty-five years later, he would be presenting me for ordination and vesting me in priestly chasuble on Pentecost Sunday, at West Hill United Church, Toronto, Ontario, May 27, 2007.

My first experience of home community Eucharist was when my brother presided at Mass in our home with our family during holiday celebrations. This brought me to a deeper sense of what Eucharist is about: family sharing, prayer, thanksgiving, community and presence. When my sister-in-law, who is a Baptist, said she believed in Christ as true presence in Eucharist, my brother gave her Communion. My mother was troubled by this because intercommunion was not acceptable in the Roman Catholic Church. Rather than continuing to upset her, our home Masses stopped. I felt a deep loss.

As a nurse, prayer and soothing touch was core to my healing work. After graduation, I worked in secular hospitals where spiritual care was not considered an important part of healing. As I worked the midnight shift, I continued to discover that medications alone were not enough to soothe and comfort my patients, so I quietly prayed with them and became ever more aware of the power that compassion, touch and prayer have for bringing patients comfort and hope.

With Vatican II, I found new hope, with liturgy and songs in English, and community participation that helped nurture me as a young mother of three children. But when I looked for community in my parish, to share life and support for family living, I found little. A friend took me to Al-Anon, where I came to see that my family struggles were related to my father's alcoholism. In Al-Anon, even more than in parish life, I discovered practical tools and a spiritual way of finding freedom from resentments, fears, struggles in relationships, and wounds from abuse. Going to meetings, I experienced a community of caring people who invited me on an honest, loving and healing journey. I found freedom and wholeness in a loving, inclusive environment.

Another friend invited me to start up an Adult Children of Alcoholics Meeting. ACA is a special group that focuses on the issues of growing up in an alcoholic home, with steps for healing the past and living fully in the present. Growing up in an alcoholic home, I knew what it meant to have lived with pain and survived, and to come to experience the deep freedom and healing of Christ's resurrection. This experience taught me the acceptance of persons in an inclusive community where all are welcome to share their holy but imperfect stories, giving strength and hope to one another. In the words of Henri Nouwen, one who has lived in pain becomes a Wounded Healer for others.

Along with this program, I participated in an intense School of Inner Healing Reflection on Scriptures, journaling, music and prayer gifted me with the healing of wounded memories and helped me to experience God's unconditional love.

I have a Bachelors Degree in Theology, a Diploma in Nursing, a Certificate in Spiritual Direction, I am a Certified Federation Christian Minister, and have fourteen years of experience in Pastoral Care in hospitals and hospice settings. I have ministered to patients, families, and staff in acute care settings. Many patients and their families taught me about unconditional love, and offered me creative ways of being present.

My husband and I owned and managed a 29-unit motel for seventeen years. I served as a contemplative in the marketplace, praying and assisting families, business persons, bus tours, senior citizens, and travelers from all over the world in their lodging needs. We served guests of all ages, backgrounds and life experiences. With my family, I became a listener of stories in our motel lobby, some of which entailed experiences I had never personally been exposed to. Even when this became a challenge, God's strength and love prevailed.

I wrote two booklets, *Meditations for Working Women* and *Meditations for Working Men*. These grew out of my interviews of guests, friends, professionals, and strangers in which they shared with me how they prayed on their particular jobs. Some did not think they prayed, but by the end of the interview, they realized that indeed they did have their own ways of praying. The interviews opened their own windows of spirituality.

Because of the patience and compassion of many on my own journey of healing, I have been given the patience to be present with mercy and compassion for others who need time to heal. The stages of a healing process differ from person to person.

My Priestly Ministry

As a Roman Catholic Womanpriest, ministry is a means of being a holder of the sacred, a witness of Light, a praying, listening presence with others as they discover their holy journeys.

I see spiritual direction as a sacred container wherein the sacrament of reconciliation takes place. In the telling of story, there is an anointing with the sign of grace and reconciliation. Freedom comes, healing comes, wisdom comes to guide their holy lives. Here, the Word is made flesh and dwells with us.

Each time I prepare a homily and the liturgy, I am reminded of God's profound action, of Christ's life, death and resurrection lived out in all of our lives again and again in human life. We are not alone despite many discomforts.

The day before my diaconal ordination, a woman approached me, saying, "You are a witness of hope. Thank you!" After I was ordained a priest, a family from my church community invited me to celebrate Eucharist in their home. Fourteen people came, sang, shared reflections on the Word, broke bread, and felt energized to go forth into their communities to share hope for the journey. At another liturgy, at the Sign of Peace, a male priest embraced me, saying, "Peace be with you, Sister Priest." What a welcomed surprise and acceptance!

Acting on this prophetic call has also brought challenges. Two close relatives have chosen to shun me unless I "stop" being a priest. I place them in the heart of God and continue to love. With each new challenge comes new grace and strength to be present, celebrate, anoint and love whomever God sends. Each day is a new day of celebrating with the Body of Christ, serving the people of story, living life on holy ground.

Some people have told me pointblank, "I stand with the pope regarding women priests," yet they look to me for listening presence, for information about the Scriptures, and for answers to religious questions.

I preside at a home Eucharist every other week with a small group. The homily is a shared reflection. Some do not wish to come to our home Eucharist, yet they continue to approach me for spiritual counseling. I visited a couple who were distressed due to an alcoholic relative. I provided information about alcoholism, gave them Al Anon literature, and talked to them about how alcoholism is a family disease. I asked them if they would like the sacrament of the sick, to which they responded affirmatively.

I make hospital and home visits, of which people are appreciative. They have expressed gratitude and invite me to return.

Mike and Irene Gallagher wrote an open letter in *The National Catholic Reporter*, on Jan. 11, 2008, in response to the articles on Roman Catholic Womenpriests, inviting a woman priest to come and celebrate with their community. On Holy Thursday, March 20, 2008, I concelebrated Eucharist with Rev. Michael Gallagher, of St. Christopher's Faith Community in Titusville, Florida, and gave the homily. The community was very supportive and welcoming. One woman came to me after the Mass saying, "Your homily touched me deeply." Many said, "Thank you. I hope you come back." Another person said that she was happy to meet a woman priest and asked for prayers.

My Road To Ordination

Preparation for this prophetic call to ordination and service as a Roman Catholic Womanpriest has taken a lifetime. My awareness of being called began while on an Ignatian retreat during Christian Unity Week in January of 1995. During an *Internship in Spiritual Direction*, I made an eight-day retreat reflecting on the Spiritual Exercises of Ignatius where I experienced a profound call to the priesthood.

My spiritual director encouraged me to work with Scripture instead of reading extra books. One night while in prayer, in a small private chapel, I heard a voice within directing me to go across the hall and take a book off the shelf. I struggled, finally walking to the bookcase. Without looking at the titles, I pulled a book, which turned out to be the *Book of Common Prayer of the Episcopal Church*, and cracked it open to "Ordination of Priest and Bishop." *What does this mean?* I wondered. My spiritual director encouraged me to continue to pray about it. I journaled, meditated and prayed for guidance. I spoke often the same words that Mary, a young woman called to be Mother of God, said at the Annunciation: *How can this be?* Before this time, I had not been involved in any reformed groups for women, nor had I ever felt called to be priest.

I wondered at times if this was about the "call to ministry" in relationship to St. Ignatius' Second Week of reflection. Yet, deep in my heart this call was a seed bursting to "I know not what." It seemed to be a call far deeper than I could imagine. If this was a call to ordination, I knew I needed more education. I had a Diploma in Nursing but I did not have an undergraduate degree, though I was 57.

Because of my leadership as President of the Hotel & Motel Association, my pastoral experience as a nurse and ministry as a spiritual director, and my eucharistic and bereavement ministry in my local parish, I received the *Aquinas Ruby Scholarship for Women Leaders Returning to School*. While at Aquinas College, I spoke of my sense of being called to the priesthood, still asking the Mary question: *How can this be?*

A religious sister and professor of Religious Studies introduced me to *Call To Action* and *Women's Ordination Conference*. In 1995, I attended my first *Call To Action* conference in Chicago, where I met many women from all over the world, sharing their stories of call; and many supportive clergy too. I was amazed that so many women were hearing the same call!

I presented a paper where I interviewed four women called to priesthood. I interviewed two married women (one of whom I'd known since first grade), a religious sister, and a single woman. They shared their calls, their experience of small faith communities, their hopes, frustrations and encouragement – which gave me hope. We had common stories of being impregnated with a call to ordination that would not leave us despite it being *contra legem*.

During a course, "The Sacrament of Eucharist," I learned the various dimensions of Eucharist from Paul Bernier's book, *Eucharist: Celebrating Its Rhythms In Our Lives.* "The five rhythms of the Eucharistic celebration are intrinsic to the liturgy." I finally felt a deep sense of meaning in my experience, which had been that of liturgy including the whole community. Some members of my family had a "private connection" which I did not experience.

I found Communion and a deeper experience of being presence through the rhythms of gathering, storytelling, the prophetic dimension, nurturing, and missioning. I presented a paper discussing the prophetic dimension, sharing various quotes of eucharistic persons who lived prophetic lives. Liturgy is all of life. Celebrating Eucharist invites us to be eucharistic people. We share the Body of Christ through giving ourselves to the Body of Christ.

I baptized at the bedside. A patient asked to go to confession, and when I offered to get her a priest, she said, "You are my priest" She shared her pain. I prayed with her a prayer of forgiveness, anointed her with oil, and she felt peace. For one family, I had a funeral service at the bedside, as the family could not afford a funeral. For another, I facilitated a funeral service at the funeral home on Holy Thursday. There were not any Catholic priests available due to parish needs.

In 1999, I filled out a survey prepared by the Women's Ordination Conference for those who felt called to ordination. My answer was "Yes!" yet I struggled over taking a stand. The "Yes" came from deep within, birthing and permeating my being! Going forward, I went through the doors as they opened. Persons from the community shared their hunger for inclusive liturgy.

I continued to serve as a spiritual care counselor, both in the hospital and for part of my beginning service at hospice. I was experiencing being priest, being presence, praying healing comforting prayer, offering compassion and having the privilege to serve others as they journeyed from this life to the next. This was being priestly, and this was loving as Christ loved. I was being Eucharist on their journeys.

Through the Women's Ordination Conference, I discovered Roman Catholic Womenpriests, an international initiative within the Roman Catholic Church. I learned of the first Roman Catholic Womenpriests ordinations in North America, on the St. Lawrence Seaway. I knew I needed to be there.

During the Women's Ordination Worldwide Conference (WOW) in Ottawa, before the ordination, women and men from all over the world gathered together sharing their visions of a Vatican II Church. We celebrated Eucharist together. Everyone was welcomed at the table, as Jesus welcomed all. I was accepted into the RCWP Program of Preparation during this conference. I didn't hear, "You can't come if...." I was reminded of the road to Emmaus, where the disciples recognized Christ in the breaking of the bread. I discovered contemplative people of God, hearing the same voice. It is time to respond in prophetic obedience to a call being spoken across the nations. God is still speaking.

When I returned home from the WOW conference, I told my husband John about my decision and acceptance into the preparation program. He was quiet at first and then responded, "It is time!" He has continued on the journey with me, my personal cheerleader.

I was ordained a deacon a year later, July 31, 2006, by Bishops Patricia Fresen, Gisela Forester and Ida Raming. We were on a chartered boat, the Majestic, on the three rivers bordering Pittsburgh, PA. Family and friends, including Rita McEachen Neal, one of the women I had interviewed for the paper I did while in college, came to celebrate this historic occasion of the first ordination in the United States.

On Pentecost Sunday, May 27, 2007, I was ordained a woman priest by Bishop Patricia Fresen at West Hill United Church in Toronto, Ontario, Canada. My sister Sally Schaden, brothers Dick, Tom, and Bob Schaden, and sister-in-law Bert Schaden, and friends who came were each moved personally by the celebration. The church was filled. I knew then that though this was a calling within me, it was a calling for the community, giving hope and encouragement to many.

God continues to open paths of Light with persons walking the road less traveled to re-imagine Christianity and to love as Jesus modeled love, where all are invited to the City of God without constraints. In God's love and grace, I journey on.

Ordained a priest: 2007, Ontario

PROPHETIC OBEDIENCE

Kathy Sullivan Vandenberg

WHEN I WAS GROWING up, I lived in the country and attended a one-room country school. No playmates were available to me during the summers so I was privileged to roam the hills and surrounding land. This meant I had plenty of time to think about religion and spiritual things. I was not able to get into town often, but my parents always took me to church. Priests were the privileged few who were able to gather around the Eucharistic Table in their ornate vestments and hold the golden vessels that contained the white wafers that were God. I always knew I was not worthy to receive Jesus because I was regularly told that I was not worthy. When I graduated from college, ministry/vocation was not in a person's everyday vocabulary. Only a male priest could have a "true vocation" because women could not be ordained.

My parents granted me a great gift when they educated me. I was the first girl to go to college in the family. Because of this I was able to become a teacher, and have taught in grade school, high school, and college. I also received a Masters in Counseling and a Masters in Divinity at St. Francis Seminary in Milwaukee, Wisconsin. I was an educator in my parish and at all of the parishes I worked at. Later I become a Professional Counselor for the State of Wisconsin. As one of my functions, I began a grief group for parents of murdered children. In addition, I am a certified trauma specialist with two thousand hours of supervision. I also am a mother, wife, and educator to my two daughters and wonderful grandson.

Another gift I bring to my ministry is an inquiring mind. I remember sitting in my theology classes at the seminary and asking questions. One in particular comes to mind: *If a priest does not have to be holy to be ordained why is the gender of the person wanting to be ordained so important?* I also asked this question: *Is there a different baptism for girls than for boys because it is by baptism that we are welcomed into the Church and given the opportunity to receive all of the sacraments?* I was told by the priest instructor that I was not to ask any more questions in class. Instead I was to write down any questions before class and give them to him. The young men were never held to that standard.

One day, while teaching, something changed for me. A young boy named Timmy brought a large box to school that held a mother turtle and dozens of turtle eggs. All day long Timmy would shout out loud, "Another one is hatching." The entire classroom would stop the activities I had planned and rush to the box. I realized that to Timmy I was truly a minister. This was the highlight of his year because he had a chance to be the special person he never could be during the regular year. I realized hat I had the power to enrich someone's life. Since then I have continued to be an educator, from grade school through graduate school. I also was a campus minister, spiritual director, counselor, and minister to the chronically mentally ill. I remain a minister as a chaplain at this time in my life.

When I graduated from high school there were roughly four options for young women: I could go to college, get married, become a secretary, or become a nurse. Although my parents were working-class people, they sacrificed much to send me to college. Becoming a priest was never something I could think about, but in the parish community, I immersed myself in the parish council, the liturgy committee, RCIA, and many other activities. I felt called to attend Mass every day, and began seeing someone for spiritual direction. One day I was talking to a Lutheran minister who asked me, "What would you like to do if you could do anything in the world you wanted?" I immediately said that I wanted to be an ordained Catholic priest. He smiled and said, "I knew you would say that because you act the same as other Lutheran women seminary students." I then asked my spiritual director the same question. He replied, "You want to be an ordained priest. You have the same call as the other male seminary students I have worked with." My life was forever changed because my call was confirmed by two respected clergy members, and I could now actively think and pray about what this was going to mean.

After attending the Women's Ordination Conference in 1978, and being invited to stand if called to ordination, I began to think about what I could do to continue to discern my calling and to work for an end to sexism in the Church of Milwaukee. Together, a number of us gathered outside the archdiocesan Cathedral an hour before the annual ordinations were to begin. We prayed for the men being ordained to the priesthood, and we also prayed for the Church to begin recognizing the call of women to be ordained. We were booed, shouted at, and had beer bottles thrown at us. The worst part was becoming "invisible" to friends, seminary teachers, and my classmates in the seminary. I had never been invisible before. It was as if one day I was sought after and recognized and the next day I did not even exist. I had a beginning knowledge how the poor and the homeless are invisible to most people. I led the prayer vigil for the next fifteen years, until the pain became too great.

The thought that I was called to priesthood was almost impossible to grasp. I felt the fire burning within me, but most times I would flee from this intense burning invitation. In 1986 I was invited to come to a meeting in Rochester, New York for women who wanted to form a community and work for the ordination of women now. The group was called RAPPORT and was a special project of the Women's Ordination Conference. Together, we discerned our call to priesthood, supported one another, and were invited by several Roman Catholic bishops to work with them on the Bishop's Pastoral on Women. These women are some of the finest, holiest, and bravest women I know. They are an important reason why I could continue on my journey. These women would not be denied. There were no obstacles too formidable. They constantly encouraged me to say *Yes* to God. As the call became stronger and stronger, I said *Yes* to God again and again, and tried in every way to become obedient to God's call. Prophetic obedience to God and primacy of conscience led me to contact Bishop Patricia Fresen and ask to be considered for ordination through Roman Catholic Womenpriests. She ordained me a priest in Pittsburgh, PA, in 2006.

Many people have contacted me and told me they are thrilled that I have become a priest. Some have been coming faithfully to eucharistic liturgies in my home. Some have invited me to have a family Eucharist. Because I had knee replacement surgery that did not go well, I was confined to home for most of nine months during 2007. Although I was limited in mobility, I baptized, witnessed marriages, heard confessions, and counseled. I have been asked to do spiritual direction and counseling for ministers in many denominations. I also have been invited to celebrate Eucharist in a small farm community. Many members of my family are thrilled that their mother and grandmother is a priest. At the ordination in Pittsburgh, my grandson introduced me and said, "This is my grandma and I love her." What more could I ask for as a recommendation? My grandson always tells his friends that his grandma is a priest. This is remarkable in itself because he is a teenager.

Some people, however, including members of my immediate family, have dismissed my ordination and refuse to talk about it. They believe that because the pope did not sanction it, the ordination did not happen. My biggest disappointment is the fact that not any of my seminary classmates or other ordained Catholic clergy in the diocese sent me cards or called to congratulate me. Fear is a big factor. The only "official" recognition I received was from my bishop, who put a full-page insert into my parish bulletin telling the parish members that I was not a priest and that I must repent. It was especially difficult for my eighty-nine-year old mother, who is a member of that parish, to read such a harsh pronouncement. My mother and I have "solved" the impasse by not talking about my ordination.

This is not a path for the faint of heart. It was and continues to be the hardest decision I have had to make. It also is a decision that gives me great peace and happiness because I know that now, by working within the Roman Catholic Church, I can help it reform and grow for my children and my grandson and for all of the other children.

My understanding of ministry continues to grow since being ordained a deacon and a priest in the Roman Catholic Womenpriests movement. Because I had experienced few women ministers and liturgies, I had a great hunger to listen to and participate in women's eucharistic liturgies. Even now I am still trying to understand what it means to be a priest. I look into a mirror and I still look the same as I did before I was ordained. I know that I am the same – but also different. I learned that in ministry the basic beliefs are constant. God's abundant grace in the Eucharist and Word are forever there. People are needed to break open the Word and to give new understanding to the meaning of community. I am a servant to the People of God. I am a willing partner in creating a new model of what it means to be Roman Catholic. And, yes, women are fit matter for the sacrament of orders.

Ordained a priest: 2006, Pittsburgh

Alice M. Iaquinta, Priest
Mary Frances Smith, Deacon

Iaquinta

Left to right:
Regina Nicolosi, Mary Frances Smith, Barbara Zeman, Kathy Redig, Alice
Iaquinta, Victoria Rue

COMING FULL CIRCLE

The Journey Back To the Beginning
Alice M. Iaquinta

I am a teacher.

I never planned on becoming a priest. The thought never occurred to me until after I graduated from the seminary.

In the last four decades, I periodically gave up on the Church. After a year spent with Quakers in 1994, sitting in prayerful silence, I began to feel the Spirit nudging me. Then I got the message, "It's time to go home." I resisted, but did return to the Catholic Church with a deep awareness of the Spirit's living presence and a solid commitment to be a Vatican II Catholic despite my increasing disillusionment over the Church's growing change of direction. Raised as an Evangelical Lutheran, I had hopefully converted to Catholicism during the Council.

Although my call had been shaped, affirmed, challenged, and changed during the six years of theological, pastoral and spiritual formation I experienced while studying for the Master of Divinity at St. Francis Seminary in Milwaukee, Wisconsin, 2000—2006, I first discerned God's call in June 1996. I was emerging out of a dark night of the soul, bereft, bewildered and broken. I was led into a contemplative life of prayer and an informal study of unfamiliar works by others, which explained my own experiences. I read the classics: *The Devout Life, The Interior Castle, The Spiritual Exercises, The Imitation of Christ, The Tao Te Ching, Centering Prayer, The Cloud of Unknowing.*

The impetus for going to seminary was my left brain noisily demanding a systematic understanding of my experiences. I had no ministerial career goal, no ecclesiological agenda, no theological stance or substance. I just wanted to know more about the tradition that I had discovered I was part of. I applied because I knew I was "supposed to," but just what I was showing up for wasn't clear to me in 2000. I had articulated a call in a 1996 letter, although I hadn't then recognized it.

My call is what T.S. Eliot describes as the journey back to where you began.

Today, my teaching has taken a decidedly spiritual turn, and students come to me about their spiritual, as well as their academic, lives. I have learned that when I completely surrender, giving up any resistance to the possible paths in front of me, the right one becomes evident. As long as I resist or rationalize, the answer is elusive. Initially I had a flawed interpretation of the call I heard, "Teach for me." I thought it meant I had to leave teaching to go into ministry in a church setting. It didn't. Everything in my life has led me to this point of convergence. All the diverse pursuits, the mistakes, the wrong turns have been threads that God has woven into the cloth of my life with which I will cloak myself as a priest.

In 1996, I was running on empty. From then until now, I have been filled up to overflowing with an abundance of knowledge, experience, and gifts to share in teaching and healing ministries, by God's grace. I am still surprised at this turn of events in my life, but grateful. I have been taken into the heart of Love.

Textual analyses of seminary self-evaluations reveal emerging themes, issues, and evidence of the Spirit's direction in my life. I can now discern the Spirit's role in my formation, as I followed God's lead in the dance of my life. The texts speak the truth of my formation to become a priest. It wasn't my idea.

My life was shifting in 1996. I had taken a break from Doctoral studies in Adult Education at the University of Wisconsin-Madison. I was deep into discernment, only at the time I didn't understand the process, the implications, or the tradition of "the call." Moving from informal to formal study, from bewilderment to enlightenment, from brokenness to wholeness, from bereftness and despair to joy, peace and hope, from uninformed to formed and informed, from unknowing to knowing and then back to unknowing, has been my journey over the last twelve years. Mine has been and is the mystical experience of purgation, illumination and union. Journey with me now, back over the last twelve years, for glimpses into how one woman's call evolved.

In June of 1996, in a letter to my doctoral advisor at UW-Madison after an eighteen-month break from studies, I wrote:

The direction I thought this Doctorate would be taking me is not the direction I am to go. My intentions had been to move into teacher pre-service and in-service education. However, more and more events have been unfolding that are leading me to Adult and Family Ministry in the Catholic Church and also outreach education with the Church's Social Issues Office. This is so surprising and overwhelming to me....

This sure wasn't on my agenda! But I guess things are unfolding just the way that they are supposed to. I am listening to my heart about the path I am to follow. I have learned that I am not in control, that I am to do God's will and that means Adult Education for the Church.... Everything I have studied has an important part to play in that work. Nothing has been for naught. As soon as I complete prelims, I will begin taking relevant coursework at St. Francis Seminary in Milwaukee, to gain a stronger theological background for the work I am being led to do. That will go slowly though because I want to finish the dissertation and graduate by June of 1997, if possible.

Well, that didn't happen. God had other ideas, and in May of 2000, on my seminary application, I wrote:

When I began my doctoral work I thought I was going to ultimately become a teacher educator.... Having completed all the doctoral coursework and begun the dissertation on "transformational learning," researched hermeneutically, I was abruptly stopped..... I had a hissy fit with God. "OK, I'm yours, I realize you don't want me teaching at the university. But you have made me what I am, a very good teacher, and a grand lover of learning. What do you want me to do?" And that's when the call crystallized. "Teach for me."... God has graced me with a fine mind, boundless energy and enthusiasm and a gift of healing through my teaching. I am to use those gifts for the rest of my life in God's service, through adult and family ministry, social justice teaching, adult formation programs, pastoral work, and healing ministries.... After keeping me in the desert from 1993 to 1998, I feel as if God has shot me from a canon since the end of '98.... I guess I am still discerning! All I know is that God's love is the thing that matters most in my life and the joy I experience in God's presence makes me desire nothing more than to be obedient in all ways. I have learned what love is. I have much to give because God has given me so much, even though I deserved so little... Thank you for considering my application.

In the first seminary self-evaluation, three years later, I wrote:

This year I have experienced the sense of really knowing what I'm talking about theologically. Today I can employ exegesis, hermeneutics and Lectio Divina in scripture study and homiletics. Three years ago I could not. I was overwhelmed because everything was new and I knew so little. I now habitually integrate theological reflection in every aspect of my life and learning. Learning about the plurality of theological expressions evolved over two millennia is one of the most captivating features of the faith for me... I struggle with theological differences and disagree with the hierarchical authority on issues of

129

justice, equality and inclusiveness. My passion for those things can lead me to impatience, annoyance, and anger, especially when statements or documents are promulgated without benefit of collegial discernment of the whole people of God.

The next year I completed my second St. Francis Seminary self-evaluation.

Affirmations in homiletic training, CPE and parish placement centered not only on intellectual competence, but on my dispositions of empathy, presence, listening, openness, passion and enthusiasm, and love of learning and teaching. I do not see myself as "special," but as uniquely gifted... However, I have become increasingly sure that I am not called to be a full time chaplain. My gifts are in teaching and learning and those are of less significance for chaplaincy tasks.... My ministry lies elsewhere.... Shaped by both Vatican II reforms and radical '60's idealism, I live ideologies of equality, inclusion and freedom rather than philosophize or theologize about them. Accepting the process of change as incremental, even glacial, has relieved some stress for me. However, that does not mean I won't continue to work as hard as I can for change, while I am alive. I know now those efforts will bear fruit in generations to come. I have come to think in time lines of centuries rather than decades... I look forward to growing in my liturgical leadership role, the focus of my growth in ministry. The gifts of leadership, communication, and teaching will be important strengths for that task.... Discernment of my call is clearer than at my last evaluation. My love for learning and teaching are part of the call. Personally, I would like to teach for the church in some capacity. Parish director seems like such an overwhelming responsibility, not one I am eager to jump into. Although I know I will be prepared for and capable of it, I just don't hunger for it. I would much rather work with a community of learners focusing on some facet of theology, spirituality, catechesis, scripture study or theological reflection. Thus, I am still open to the Spirit's direction; I have no particular goal. I accept that my future goal will unfold as God wills.

In December of 2004, I submitted the final Integration Paper for a Theological Reflection Seminar.

Empowering students to live more relationally- healthy lives has transformed into empowering parishioners to recognize and use their gifts to live more participative lives in the parish.... "Bridge" was my assigned password, a metaphor for transition. Everything in my life has prepared me for this crossing. But this has not been a one-way movement over the bridge. Seminary education in ethics and pastoral counseling has also informed my teaching in the college classroom.

Knowing that I am on this bridge to ministry has been an impetus for students to talk to me about their spiritual lives. I have come to think of this as "hallway ministry." The spirituality that I bring to the classroom has opened up the space for students to address issues like forgiveness and the spirituality of parenting, marriage, and work. Ethics informs the critical thinking course in deep ways. I am still not sure that I am supposed to go into parish ministry full time so the bridge metaphor is helpful for me to think of myself as being able to go back and forth and as being a bridge for others in their own spiritual development no matter where they are. I can easily move between the roles of teacher and preacher, student to leader, from theory to practice... The intuitiveness I have about people who are in need or have wounded souls usually opens floodgates of healing tears when I invite them to share their burdens. The listening and sharing become sacramental... As a person and as a minister, what I have learned about myself is that I am ready. I am prepared. I am capable. I love ministry, warts and all. It is not so different from teaching.... I might consider pursuing pastoral counseling in ministry.

Finally, in April of 2006, I concluded the last self-evaluation for the seminary formation program.

I see myself as ready and willing, prepared and excited to begin the next leg of my journey. Being able to do something doesn't necessarily mean I am called to do it. I am now able to choose instead of trying to do everything.... I am a lot less naïve than when I entered seminary, which has not led to cynicism but to a deeper commitment to justice and equality in the world and the Church. Being a bridge for others into the difficult, murky and befuddling complexities of theology and the faith is a strength. I have always been an innovator and frequently ahead of the times, but don't let discouragement about the slowness of change keep me from moving forward. My biggest weakness has been in not understanding the meaning of the movement of the Spirit in my life as it was occurring. I am better at that now, but will continue to work at being a better listener to God's direction... Discernment makes clear I am to teach for God. It was the call I actually heard from the voice with no sound in May of 2000, following a four-year delay after becoming intuitively aware of the call. I dragged my feet, avoided and ignored it. But the hound of heaven was relentless until I applied to the seminary. I had to be willing to detach from teaching to consider ministry and that was hard for me to do because I so love teaching and learners. But once I took that step, every formation experience and all the academic preparation reinforced that I was to teach.... Jesus Christ is my teaching model: a storyteller, whose practical application of the Good News used people's lives as their textbook. Jesus taught in the synagogue, but also wherever he was and wherever people came to him for guidance, answers, and healing. While I will formally teach in the Church, parish and classroom, my ministry will also happen as I walk through life, encountering others on their journeys. I think of it as an "out and about" ministry.... 'Twas grace that brought me here and only by God's amazing grace that I was able to persevere. It has been daunting. I am glad to say, it is finished, knowing full well that it is just the beginning of what lies mysteriously ahead. I am ready.

The final three words of my self-evaluation are the very words that I uttered with joy when ordained: "Here I am. I am ready." To have my closest seminary friend tell me weeks after graduation that I needed to be ordained came as a complete surprise. Several weeks followed that intense conversation, filled with too many incidents to relate here, all confirming that the Spirit had prepared me to answer the call to priesthood. I discerned one more year with clergy, classmates, family, friends, and parishioners. All confirmed my call. RCWP became the path, provided by the Spirit, to ordination. I minister now at a parish, Jesus Our Shepherd, north of Milwaukee, Wisconsin, with six married priests. I continue to teach at a public college, but now I teach love and justice, the foundational Gospel values, in Marriage and the Family and Applied Ethics courses that were offered for the first time the year I was ordained. I am living my thesis, "The Spirituality of Teaching and Learning." Years of discerning and trusting proved that Grace does indeed build on nature. I have arrived at where I began.

I am a teaching priest.

Ordained a priest: 2007 Minneapolis

AN INTERVIEW WITH REGINA NICOLOSI

Mary Frances Smith

M Y NAME IS MARY FRANCES Smith. I am a registered nurse with a Master of Arts Degree in Theology. And I am an ordained Roman Catholic womandeacon on the discernment path toward priesthood. But it is not about myself that I write. Rather, it is about the person who played a major role in my embarking on this journey. On May 29, 2006, I had the privilege of interviewing Regina Nicolosi for my Master's thesis, "The River and the Rock: Women Shaping Church." During that interview, Regina shared the story of her life as it pertains to her spiritual path, the path that led her to Roman Catholic priesthood. At the time of the interview she was, herself, a Roman Catholic woman deacon. Shortly after our interview, Regina traveled to Switzerland in the company of her husband, Charles, her children, and some of her friends. On June 24, 2006, in a ceremony on Lake Constance, Regina was ordained a Roman Catholic womanpriest. This is the story of her own amazing journey, as she told it to me.

In a little Minnesota river town, a 64-year-old woman invites me into her home. Her hair is white, her eyes hazel, her gaze direct. Her demeanor is quiet and self-contained. At the same time, there is a distinct feeling of openness and welcome. She has never met me before, yet she is willing, even eager, to talk with me about her life in the Roman Catholic Church. That life is groundbreaking because she, along with a small group of Roman Catholic women, is on a path toward ordination to priesthood. Already she has been ordained a deacon during a ceremony on the St. Lawrence River in 2005. I begin asking my questions. She listens attentively, and then in a soft German accent, in a voice with a timbre of intensity, she begins to speak. She grew up in another small river town on the Rhine in Germany. She was the youngest of three children, having two older brothers. Hers was a devout Catholic family. She can recall incorporating officiating at Mass into her play, using berries as hosts when she was five or six. She had no awareness that females could not do this. Later, with no female role models, the practice faded away. Growing up, she loved church ritual and participated whenever she could. Along the way, certain adults advocated for her participation, in spite of her age and gender. These might have otherwise been barriers.

Although she describes herself as "Daddy's girl," Regina most often mentions her mother, who emerges as a strong advocate for Regina. Her mother was manic-depressive. A deeply spiritual woman and very loved by her family, including her two brothers who became Jesuit priests, she was proud to have been educated as a teacher. But then her own mother (Regina's grandmother) committed suicide, and she was called home to run her mother's household. Eventually, she married and was drawn into responsibilities for her own family. Regina thinks that her mother's loss of opportunity to use her teaching degree contributed to her depression. Even so, Regina's mother supported her regarding opportunities to learn. She insisted that Regina go to the same school her older brothers had attended. In those days, academically gifted boys went to gymnasium, where the classical languages, Greek and Latin, were included in the curriculum. Around the time Regina became eligible, gymnasium opened to girls and Regina's mother said, "You will go to the same school where your brothers go." Regina says, "I had a lot of issues with my mother, even when she died, but the older I get, the more deeply I understand her...and now I look at my daughters, living to their fullest..."

Throughout her life, Regina continued to be interested in religion. Her adolescence was a time of awakening, learning about the Holocaust and world poverty and hunger. Priesthood was never considered an option, of course. "There were no role models. I did not want to be a nun. I wanted to marry and have children." She also wanted to be an architect, a natural route for her to pursue since her family had a construction business. "I just had the need to go into a man's world to some degree. I thought, I can do that too." In this case, becoming an architect did not work out. There were many applicants competing for a few openings in universities and she was not able to get in. I point out to Regina that she is building a structure of another sort, referring to her work to change the place of women in the Church. She laughs. "Building structures has always been an interest of mine."

Regina attended Frankfurt University during the 1960's, a time of great social change. Friends were leaving the Church to join student social movements. She came close to losing her Catholic faith. "But I had a very wise student priest who introduced me to the Catholic Left, forerunners of liberation theology." These people opened for her the area of social justice. She prepared to teach, majoring in history with a minor in German and religion, and earning a certificate to teach religion. "One of the questions that I had on my religion exam was this new concept of collegiality, what it meant…looking at the hopes we had at that time." She refers to Vatican II. "I remember there was a young woman who wrote a paper on women's ordination. I remember thinking, "Well, that's odd…but again it was obviously a little thought that was there."

Regina had been teaching for two years when she took a trip to New York City, where two very significant things happened. There she met the man who would become her husband. It was also there that, browsing in a bookstore, she found a pamphlet about the conference of Catholic bishops in Medellin. She had again encountered liberation theology, and her interest grew. Eventually, Regina had a family. There was little time for formal study. As her children grew older, an intellectual hunger awakened in her. During that time, her husband became a deacon in the church. Working alongside her husband in this process, "I was gung-ho with all the preparation." At his ordination, Regina was allowed to robe him, but that was all. "I began to think, 'Why am I not allowed to do this also?' And so at the ordination, I think that's when I really had a first inclination that I would want to be ordained myself. I realized that I could not be ordained." She recalls a feeling of emptiness and deep sadness, and a sense of being treated unjustly. It seemed to her that women needed more education to be taken more seriously. She earned a Master of Arts degree in pastoral studies and found the experience wonderful. But when it came time to find a job in ministry, churches were looking for priests.

Currently, Regina is a chaplain in a long-term care facility, and she has also worked with boys in a corrections facility. She holds prayer services and distributes communion, but will not consecrate hosts until she is ordained a priest. Her local Catholic church will not openly give her the consecrated hosts, but she can obtain them from the local Episcopal church.

Our conversation shifts to her faith journey. She speaks with passion about her evolving image of God, which over time has broadened from "God as male" to a God that incorporates a female aspect. We speak of Mary Daly's quote, "If God is male, then the male is god." Hearing Mary Daly speak once, she had been shocked by Daly's apparent hostility toward men, but she also grew in her awareness of how male behavior is greatly determined by male privilege. We turn back to Regina's growing awareness of the feminine aspect of God. "One of my greatest shifts happened when I discovered the Black Madonna. While some feminist theologians wish to hold the image of 'Mary our sister,' I suggest that Mary images the Great Mother Goddess." I mention the Canaanite goddess, Ashara. "Exactly! She exists in many guises. In Israel they were just so close to Ashara."

Regina considers women's ordination in various parts of the world. "The ground breaking started in Europe. There are a few feminist theologians who are bridge builders, but the movement is strongest in the United States. I think that we have a body of highly educated nuns in this country who have kept this Church going in a progressive direction. In this country more people go to church. Most of Europe is more secular. In Latin America I don't know where it's going to go. Liberation theology is there, but the Church doesn't foster it anymore. Ultimately, if God encompasses male and female, our priesthood needs to be male and female also."

We speak of the barriers to priesthood for women, the greatest being the idea that the priest is *in persona Christi*. This, says Regina, is another way of saying that the woman is lesser. She refers to the patristic teachings regarding the fall of Eve and the impact of those teachings on women. One of Regina's reasons for being ordained is "to bring a woman's body up to the altar." She recalls how, in 2002, she first heard about women being ordained. A friend called her from Germany. "Did you hear? They ordained seven women—the Danube Seven!" These women were not the first. In communist Czechoslovakia, a small number of women, including Ludmila Javorova, had been secretly ordained as Roman Catholic priests (probably with the approval of the Vatican) in an effort to keep alive a dying Church. Later, the Vatican would excuse Ludmila from her priesthood (Halter 9-11). In 2001, Mary Ramerman, was ordained by a bishop in the Old Catholic Church, in Rochester, New York (Bonavoglia 239-256). Then in 2002 came the Danube Seven. And in 2005, there was an ordination of Roman Catholic womenpriests and deacons on the St. Lawrence River.

Regina described a number of different stances being taken by Roman Catholic women toward ordination of women. There is the group that waits for Vatican approval, working now for women to be accepted as deacons. There are those like Mary Ramerman who will choose to be ordained by bishops in the Old Catholic Church. Others believe that there is no need for hierarchy or the laying on of hands by bishops, and who choose to be ordained by their community. Some, like theologian Elizabeth Schüssler Fiorenza, believe that the current hierarchical structure is so corrupt that any woman ordained within that structure will also be corrupted. There are those who want to remain in the Catholic Church but believe that some of the laws of the Church are wrong. They maintain a *contra legem* stance within the Church. This is the group of which Regina is a part. She emphasizes that Roman Catholic Womenpriests do not wish to be a splinter group, but are carefully maintaining the line of apostolic succession back to Peter by making sure that ordinations are always performed by ordained bishops. "We're Catholics. We are not opposing the Church, but are opposing an unjust law." She says that they are also trying to change the model of Church to a more inclusive, ecumenical one, accepting married clergy and ordination of gays and lesbians. "There are some in the movement who say that all we need to do is change canon law from ordaining only male persons, but I think that there is more that we need to do."

That "more" includes the area of social justice. "We need to enrich and open the Church up, to be more aware of the oppression of the poor. If you live with oppression [as women in the church have], if you understand that there is injustice being done to you, there are several ways to react. You can be co-opted into the system and just say, 'Okay, now I am the priest and have the power' (and that happens often to groups that move up). Or you can also bring that memory and say, 'Now we need to crack open the door and bring greater inclusivity to more people and let them come in from that place of poverty.' That is what the Eucharist is all about. It has become clear to me that you cannot come to the table and not bring with you the realization of how many people are not fed out there: spiritually, yes, but also physically."

"One of the things that women can bring to this Church is that they are collaborative and bring more of the experience of everyday life, not just the intellectual aspects, the dogma, the hierarchy." Regina includes in this group the women who support the status quo. "I have met many strong and intelligent women, some of whom have feelings very similar to mine, who really want to work with the Church, who don't think it needs to change, and who are comfortable. I really think that they bring a tremendous amount of good to the community and are doing the work. I hope that they will look on their work as important gifts of women."

Since her diaconal ordination, Regina has been asked by her local archbishop to refrain from receiving communion. She has been warned that if she does not repent she will be excommunicated. It is in the relationship between the Roman Catholic women's movement and the church hierarchy that one encounters the river as it affects the rocky banks. We reflect on the apparent power and passion of the hierarchy's resistance to the movement. "I do believe," she says, "there is a

137

resistance to sexuality and that the sexual ethic of the Church is warped and stuck. In theology classrooms with males, feminist theologians may not be taken seriously in debates with men." For the hierarchy, it seems, it's the female body that is the barrier to acceptance of the value of female intellect.

I ask Regina if she perceives any disconnect between Jesus' teachings and values, the teachings of the Church, and the practices of its members. If so, what does she do with this awareness? "There is a huge disconnect, even if one looks at the outer structures." She refers to the opulence of the Vatican. "Have you seen pictures of the new pope in his red slippers? There's a disconnect between this and the core of my belief, which is that Jesus came to create a table community of equals. It's Elizabeth Schüssler Fiorenza who called it a discipleship of equals. Jesus invited everyone to that table. He didn't ask if you were a sinner, or if you were a man or a woman, or if you held a high position. As a matter of fact, he said, 'Do not go by your position.' And yet, this Church says that you must be made a certain way [to be a priest]. This even before what it means to be a priest is discussed. Eventually, there may be a different model of priesthood. Why does a person need a doctorate to celebrate the Eucharist, to be called?

"And what do I do with this process? I think a lot of it is just so big that you don't want to deal with it. And I have humbly accepted that I can only bring change about in small areas. But I think the other thing I do is join with other like-minded people and nourish and feed each other, fighting some of the small battles in my part of the world. I can distribute food (spiritual, emotional and actual) as much as I can. Otherwise the issues are so huge and overwhelming."

I am reminded of something I heard the theologian, Elizabeth Johnson, CSJ, say when asked what each of us can do in the face of social injustice. She responded, "Work in your own part of the vineyard."

"In my part of the vineyard," echoes Regina. "And for me, my part of the vineyard right now is women's ordination. It's a small area, but so…"

Regina was ordained a priest: 2006 Lake Constance
The author was ordained a deacon: 2008 Winona

Juanita Cordero, Priest
(Merlene) Olivia Doko, Priest
Kathleen Strack Kunster, Priest

Doko left, Cordero right

Left to right:
Olivia Doko, Kathleen Kunster, Juanita Cordero, Dana Reynolds and Victoria Rue.

139

DOORS CLOSED AND DOORS OPEN

Juanita Cordero

M Y CALL TO MINISTRY began when I was about six-years old. I vividly remember playing priest in our backyard, handing out Necco Wafers as communion to the neighborhood kids. But I could not be a priest because I was a female. All priestly dreams were tucked away.

After high school, I entered the Sisters of the Holy Names in Los Gatos, CA. There I got as close to the altar as I could by becoming the sacristan for the community, while also teaching in their many schools across California. Throughout ten years of service, during which I prepared children for their first Holy Communion and the sacraments of Reconciliation and Confirmation, led the music for the children's Masses, and planned many retreats for the women in the parishes, I kept hearing a call from God to leave my community and serve in a different way.

That was not the easiest thing to do, as I had no money and no place to go. Then a Jesuit brother told me of a teaching position in one of the Jesuit parish schools in Arizona. Putting my total trust in God, I applied, and was given the job before I left the convent. The diocese of Phoenix provided me a free apartment until I could get settled and begin to make it on my own. I continued to lead family liturgies in the parish and worked with the children preparing for their first Communion.

What lay ahead of me was a mystery that would slowly unfold.

In 1971, I married my husband Don Cordero, a former Jesuit, and was immediately kicked out of the parish. The pastor "excommunicated" me, and my teaching contract was terminated. Needless to say, neither of us had a job, as Don too was told to pack his bags and leave his parish in Santa Clara. However, we managed to return to California, and together raised a family of five children.

Music and liturgies were very much a part of my call to ministry, so Don and I began one of the first music groups at the Mission Church at the University of Santa Clara. Don led the group every three weeks, while I played the bass and helped plan the many liturgies to follow with the presiding priest and members of that community. Our group grew in numbers. We held practice sessions at our house every Saturday before leading the music at Mass on that following Sunday. Many of the same members participated in a prayer group we started, which lasted more than thirty years until some died or moved away.

In 2003, Don and I visited his nephews in Chicago, where we attended liturgy at an Episcopal church. There I met my first woman priest. She seemed so natural in presiding over the Eucharist. I again felt the call to the priesthood, but this wasn't possible in the Catholic Church so I dismissed the idea very quickly. Besides, I was teaching full time at De Anza College, and I'm no "spring chicken," as they would say.

After Don retired from doing music at the Santa Clara Mission Church, I happened to attend St. Mark's Episcopal Church in the area. There I witnessed another woman priest celebrating the Eucharist. She invited me to attend her liturgy, and soon I became a Eucharistic minister to her congregation. This continued for four years.

One afternoon in 2004, members of the Roman Catholic Womenpriest movement met at our house with their mentors. Don had agreed to be a mentor to Victoria Rue. I listened to their stories and realized that my call to priesthood was surfacing again. I would wake up in the middle of the night thinking about it. I kept saying, "No, God, this can't be happening. I'm too old for another life change." But the people in our prayer group encouraged me to answer God's call. So I had more, and longer conversations with God, and finally said, "If you want me to do this, I will write to Bishop Patricia Fresen and see what happens." I was accepted into the program.

Now what?

During the summer of 2005, I traveled across the United States with many women on what was know as the "Witness Wagon," visiting places that had been empowered by other women such as Susan B. Anthony. There I had a chance to talk to Patricia Fresen, who related her story of South Africa and apartheid and how she was jailed for opposing discrimination against black children and their families in her school. She turned to me and said, "This was an unjust law that needed to be broken. The refusal of the Vatican to ordain women to the priesthood is an unjust law that needs to be broken." Women should be allowed to be ordained. I knew at that moment that I was on a new journey, a journey towards priesthood. It felt so right.

Another life-changing experience came when my husband and I traveled to Tibet with Michael Saso, a former Jesuit. This was a spiritual pilgrimage, which took us into the monasteries to chant with the nuns and monks and receive special blessings from their revered lamas. Studying Buddhism has deepened my faith in Catholism.

In 2006, I was ordained a deacon in Pittsburgh. I began a house church with my husband Don and Kathleen Kunster, who had been ordained a priest in Pittsburgh. On July 22, 2007, I was ordained a priest at the La Casa in Santa Barbara.

Following my priestly ordination, I was asked to leave my Episcopal community. I was told I could no longer serve on the altar. They have some canon that prohibits clergy from another denomination to serve with them. I had served there when I was a deacon; nothing was mentioned about this regulation until after my ordination to priesthood. I miss the community, but realized it was time to move on.

I had the privilege of concelebrating with Bishop Peter Hickman in Orange County one Sunday morning. When I arrived at his church, which is in a shopping center, I was welcomed by many of his parishioners. Before the service began, a community member was going to talk about what it meant to be Catholic. What impressed me most was how the community was involved in the liturgy, and that the priest was there to serve and be served by its members. The priests received communion last, given to them by one of the parishioners. The priests who serve with Bishop Hickman are married and take turns celebrating with him.

I have years of experience in serving the people of God. I am very fortunate to have been taught theology by many of the top Jesuit theologians from Alma College in the early 1960's. Their Jesuit thinking and training allowed me to understand the changes of Vatican II and implement them into my daily life. I have a Masters in Human Development and at the present time I am pursuing a Masters in Theology with an emphasis on feminine ministry. I also have a nursing degree, and have studied Reiki, Ayurvedic medicine, and other healing modalities.

Our small Magdala Community has grown from six to around 25 members. When it was time to be ordained a priest, the group called my name and laid hands on me to send me forth. After ordination, I had the privilege of celebrating the Eucharist for our 36th wedding anniversary, then presiding over the funeral Mass of my husband, who died from Prostate Cancer shortly afterwards. On December 1, 2007, during our regular liturgical celebration, I asked the members if they would anoint Don after the Mass. Amazingly, each person bent over Don, gave his or her personal inspiration, and then, with the oil provided, laid hands on him and blessed him. After the last blessing, Don, his body wracked in pain, blessed all the members of our community.

This is what community is all about. I will continue to serve as a celebrant with Kathleen Kunster in our house church, and preside at weddings, anointing, and prayer services.

Ordained a priest: 2007, Santa Barbara

FROM RESENTMENT TO PEACE

A Story of Hope
(Merlene) Olivia Doko

F OLLOWING YEARS OF HOPE, often mixed with periods of near despair, a way opened for me to realize my dream of becoming an ordained Roman Catholic priest. Early in 2005, through a series of referrals, I was brought into contact with Roman Catholic Womenpriests, headquartered in Bavaria, which accepted my application to enter its program of preparation for ordination. In the summer of 2006, I was ordained to the priesthood in Pittsburgh, Pennsylvania, by three female bishops.

My story did not begin, nor has it ended, with my ordination.

The journey towards priesthood involved an interior awakening to my call and the simultaneous recognition of the call by other persons close to me, including my family and ordained priests. Persons began to speak to me about priesthood and women's ordination, referring to me as a priest, seeking me out for reconciliation with God through open confession of sins, turning to me to lead them in prayer and worship, asking me to anoint them and to pray with them for healing. I have experienced many memorable moments in this regard.

One moment, especially treasured, occurred in 1978 during a season of ministry behind the Iron Curtain. During a visit to her village, my then 80-year old mother-in-law, Sima Doko, who had never been more than ten miles from her home in what was known at the time as Yugoslavia (now known as Bosnia-Herzegovina), asked me to anoint and pray with a dying villager as no parish priest could be found to administer the sacrament for the sick and the dying. Sima did not know how to read or to write; but that deeply spiritual woman knew how to read the signs of the times and she knew how to read my heart and to cultivate seeds sown there by the Spirit. Whenever I pause to review the steps leading and calling me to ordination, I always remember the role that Sima played.

For a long time, I denied hearing a call to priesthood because I was focused on the "impossibility" of the call for a woman within the Roman Catholic Church. It was during my graduate studies in theology in the late 1980's that I could no longer deny the call God had planted deep within me. While participating in a future imaging process in one of my classes, I discovered and named that my greatest dream was to serve as a priest within the Roman Catholic Church. From that day forward, I began to work toward the possibility of ordination for women, joining the Women's Ordination Conference in the USA, deepening my personal spiritual and theological formation and education, listening to the Spirit in contemplation, and feeling the pain of being denied the official sacrament of Sacred Orders. I was longing to say, "Here I am. I am ready."

I sought opportunities to express my hopes and joys and pains around the issue of women's ordination and women's roles in the church. One opportunity was an invitation to address the Council of Priests in my diocese, where I and other members of a study committee were asked to speak regarding the feasibility of instituting in the diocese a Permanent Diaconate preparation program open to women as well as men. Partial content of that address was as follows:

My Brothers and Sisters in Christ Jesus,

I am here today in peace...but I am not here in a peace that is free of pain. In prayer, I have labored long in order to discern the words to be spoken forth from my heart to your hearts.

My prayer, in this season of jubilee, has been like the prayer of "a woman in childbirth, who knows her hour has come," and who, in an interior night, waits with great sighs and cries for the appearance of her child. That child's name will be "Justice."

My prayer, in this season of jubilee, has been like the prayer of an old crone, who having dug the earth and planted seeds with her hands, presses her face to the ground in order to hear the sounds and smell the fragrances of new growth from within the heart of the soil. That soil is the church and that new growth is freedom born of equality.

To pray these prayers, in this season of jubilee, has been to enter with Jesus Christ...who remains the same yesterday, today and forever...into that time and place before humankind formed "knowledge" of false divisions between the male and the female. I believe it is in that sacred space that a vision in which to live and breathe and move can be found. I believe that it is only in movement from that sacred space that a movement toward justice can be most fully initiated.

The vision I hold in my heart, the vision that I carry forth, for the present moment in our diocesan history is a just process which will honor the call of men and of women for a deeper life in service to God and to the church, especially to the poor and to all persons without a voice. Without a just process, any process, no matter how noble its goals, will not bear the lasting fruit of a just result.

The vision I hold in my heart, the vision that I carry forth, for the future life of the church is a community of believers, a community of men and women, equally carrying and breaking open the Word, Who is Jesus, to one another and to all who arrive hungry at their table.

Over time, I came to understand and believe that an entirely new paradigm of priesthood is being called and created for Catholic men and women. I do not believe that a more feminist model simply can be superimposed over the current patriarchal model. Rather, I believe a new model of priesthood is being birthed. I believe a cosmic shift is occurring on multiple levels and that women's ordination, as it is now being manifested through programs and organizations such as RCWP, is part of this cosmic shift.

Actively participating in this shift is a challenge; but it is one filled with much joy and peace as well as opportunity for growth. It is a task undertaken in response to the needs of the People of God, including, but not limited to, those who continue to support me with love, prayers and words of encouragement as I am invited to become more fully the priest I have been created to be.

Early in preparation for ordination through RCWP, I realized I needed first to recognize and then to move to a place of freedom and peace, a place beyond the angry and negative feelings within me regarding the church. If not recognized and released, I knew those same feelings had the potential to hinder my becoming a loving Christ-bearer in the world. To assist me in this process, in the spring of 2005, my spiritual director invited me to participate in a spiritual exercise, which would allow me to name what I resented, demanded and appreciated about the circumstances surrounding the church's stand on women's ordination. The exercise bore good fruit; but it was not an easy one for me as I was reluctant to use words such as "resent" and "demand" when I preferred to use words such as "am uncomfortable with" and "seek." Here is what I wrote:

Resent

I resent that the patriarchical structure of the Roman Catholic Church does not give full voice and opportunity to women.

I resent that many priests and bishops who, knowing it is wrong and unholy not to give full voice and opportunity to women, do nothing to correct this injustice, but rather continue to allow women to suffer...holding back just words and actions out of fear of sharing their power with women and/or out of fear of retaliation and humiliation by Rome and/or by the more conservative members of the laity and clergy.

I resent that many priests and bishops, once open to working for change within the church in regards to assisting women to have a full voice and opportunity, are now betraying and denying the Christocentric nature of women by using weak "theological" arguments and logic to deny and betray not only women, but themselves as well by denying and betraying that which they truly believe.

I resent the negative and unhealthy effect these actions/inactions have on the psyche of the priests and bishops, on the souls and spirits of women, and on the life of the whole church...on the very Body of Christ, which is continually being wounded by the injustice and abuse suffered by women, including by those women who are unaware of their abuse and the injustice done to them, all over the world.

I resent that these same priests and bishops, who by their inaction and their closing of doors to women have helped create an environment that has abandoned and led many women to work from outside, rather than inside, the church to bring about healing and freedom for themselves as women and for the church as a whole. I further resent that these same priests and bishops now complain and claim falsely that those women who have chosen to work from outside the church structure to bring about its and their healing and freedom have abandoned the church when it is sick.

As a woman I feel anger and I feel pain and sorrow about this situation...not only for myself, but also for all women as well as for the church. On a personal level I hurt deeply because I have been and am being betrayed, denied and misunderstood by priests whom I had considered good friends. Likewise, I resent that I at times have allowed myself to react rather than respond to their acts of betrayal, denial and misunderstanding toward me. Even as I understand the struggles of these priests and have compassion for and love these men, I cannot condone their current attitude toward and inaction on behalf of me and women in general...nor do I condone any failure on my part to respond from a place of wisdom and vision whenever I have been victimized by their attitudes and inactions.

If the priests and bishops do not or cannot find the courage to stand up for us women and make a way for us to be invited into the *inner circle of community, then we women must be open to new ways in which to create avenues for the Holy Spirit to bring about justice for women and to create effective ways for administering healing to the Church from outside its current structure. I personally must do this for all the reasons outlined above...and I must do so because for me to remain in a sick structure that won't allow me to help heal it from within not only exacerbates the sickness of the structure, but causes me to become ill as well. The physician must heal herself...then be an instrument of healing to others.*

For me to seek ordination to the Roman Catholic priesthood from outside the current church structure, while at the same time knowing that my ordination will be an outward sign of the deep and loving connection I feel with the heart of Christ Jesus and of the Catholic Church, is the greatest prophetic action I can take at this time in my spiritual journey. At the same time this action, born of my faithfulness to God, is my positive and loving response to the deepest place of union with the Holy Trinity within me...and it is my offering not only of all that I am as gift to God; but it also is a pouring out of myself with love for the good of the Church and the world. I can make no other response than to take the risks, including the risk of painful losses of precious friendships, inherent in my decision to be ordained to the priesthood. I am who I am and I will be who I will be...who I have been created to be...even before I was formed in my mother's womb. I am becoming who I will become.

Let those who have ears, hear. Let those who have eyes, see. Let those who have minds, understand.

Demand

I demand a forum consisting of men and women, clergy and laity alike, be established worldwide by the Vatican in the Roman Catholic Church in which the issue of women being given full voice and opportunity, including ordination to the priesthood, can be discussed and considered in a mutually respectful and informed manner by persons on all sides of the issue.

I demand a new and healthy model of ordained priesthood, one that includes men and women, whether married or single, whether heterosexual or homosexual, be created and established in the Roman Catholic Church.

I demand that the declaration of excommunication be removed from all women who have been ordained to the Roman Catholic Priesthood. Likewise I demand that any bishop who has suffered excommunication for ordaining women to the Roman Catholic

148

Priesthood, be reinstated into full fellowship and faculties within the Church.

I demand that the Vatican of the Roman Catholic Church end its reign of tyranny with its inherent stifling of spiritual growth, change and intellectual exploration not only in the matter of women's ordination, but also in all arenas of theological and doctrinal inquiry.

I demand that the great wealth of information contained in the historical records at the Vatican be disseminated to all those who ask to review and receive it.

There is a great shift taking place in the cosmos as all creation groans and cries out for both the sons and the daughters of God to take their rightful places in God's community of faith. A new model of priesthood is emerging; and its riches are yet to be discovered and defined. God is doing something new and is making all things new...including the Roman Catholic Priesthood, which will include both men and women.

Appreciate

I appreciate the courageous efforts by prophetic men and women, working both inside and outside the current church structure, to awaken the hearts of all the People of God to the need for justice and equality and full voice and opportunity for women in the Roman Catholic Church.

I appreciate those courageous priests and bishops who, at great risk to themselves, support the ministry of women and the call of women to ordination in the Roman Catholic Church.

I appreciate all those men and women who have died and gone before me, marked with the sign of faith, who have been and continue to be great beacons of light and truth calling men and women to allow their hearts of stone to be turned into hearts of flesh concerning the needs of women to be treated equally in all aspects of church ministry.

I appreciate the testimony of the examples of Jesus when he embraced and raised women to a more valued status in society and in the faith community. I appreciate Jesus.

I appreciate those sacred words of scripture not recorded, even purposely omitted, in the writings of the New Testament which are nonetheless marked and inspired by the Spirit of God.

One day the patriarchical structure of the church, not the church itself, will crumble. Justice will reign...even rain down...for women in the Roman Catholic Church; and when it does, the mercy of God will flow and fill and flood the Temple.

Amen and Amen
Alleluia

Peace

Letting go of anger and resentment, letting go and letting God, which is an on-going process, has brought me much peace within my priesthood. I pray that same peace is radiated with compassion and that it continues to grow within me.

I peacefully accept that being ordained "outside" the structure, but "inside" the heart of the Roman Catholic Church has placed me at risk with the structure. With peace I have received the news that the Vatican has declared that I, by being ordained to the Roman Catholic priesthood, have been excommunicated *latae sententiae*. I do not accept this punishment. It is as unjust as is the unjust code in Canon Law, which prohibits the ordination of women. I do not accept my excommunication as valid. It is my priesthood that is valid. I believe I must live fully who I am and be on the outside of myself who I am on the inside of myself, a priest called to serve the People of God. I have no desire to leave the church; and I continue to see myself as a vital member of the church, seeking to awaken the church to the prophetic call of God in this current period of history.

My present ministry as a priest is expressed in two major arenas: 1) being a pastoral presence to and with others as I administer the Sacraments of the Church; 2) serving as Program Coordinator for both the Western and the Central Regions of the USA. In the latter expression, it is my privilege to recruit and mentor women through the preparation program process as they move toward ordination to the diaconate and the priesthood.

These ministries are held in balance with my care for my family and my life of prayer. I am a Camaldolese Benedictine Oblate; and the spiritual rhythm of embracing my role as a "monk in the world" helps to sustain me and to build my relationships with God, self and others.

My ordination is an outward sign of the deep and loving connection I feel with the heart of the Catholic Church; and receiving the sacrament of ordination has been the greatest prophetic action I have taken to date in my spiritual journey. This action, which I experience as being born of faithfulness to God, is for me a positive and loving response to the deepest place of union with the Divine within me. It is an offering of all that God has given me, hopefully for the good of the Church and the world.

I believe that one day the patriarchical structure of the church will crumble. Justice will reign...even rain down...for women in the Roman Catholic Church; and when it does, the mercy of God will flow and fill and flood the Temple With every woman who is ordained to the priesthood, the heavens open to pour forth this rain. I believe this rain is part of a latter day rain of harvest. May God be glorified.

Ordained a priest: 2006 Pittsburgh

BIOGRAPHY OF A PRIEST

Kathleen Strack Kunster

I GREW UP PRIMARILY IN California. My family had been through the Great Depression and World War II, and we were living in Hawaii as Navy dependents when I was in first grade during the Korean War. We thought we might stay in Hawaii the following year and I kept asking to attend the Catholic school. But the following year we moved to Los Angeles and I started second grade.

Los Angeles public schools had a "release time" arrangement in which children could go to religious education for one hour a week. I was presented with a list of three churches that offered religious education. I chose "Catholic" with great assurance but no understanding of why I was choosing it. I loved catechism from the first moment. I received First Communion the following spring. Like 99 percent of the other women priests, and possibly most Catholic children, I played mass when I was a child. However, the boy with whom I played mass, although a year younger, already knew that girls couldn't be priests. So I had to watch as he pretended to celebrate mass. I already had leanings toward priesthood.

By the time that I was in seventh grade, I knew without any doubt that I wanted to be a priest. The associate pastor of the parish made an announcement at morning mass, saying, "Anyone who thinks he has a vocation to the priesthood should come and talk to me." I remember thinking two things: 1) "he" included everyone according to our teachers; 2) I was honor-bound to talk to him about my vocation despite the fact that he was very intimidating. So after mass I walked up to him and said I thought I had a vocation to the priesthood. He said that women could not be priests. I asked why and he said, "Because they can't be fathers to the people." I thought, "I can be a mother to the people."

I considered religious life, but it was never a fit. I entered college, worked, had a family, and eventually became a certified public accountant. I began doing lay ministry in my parish in 1981. In 1988 I had a serious bout with cancer; and the following year I was poisoned with an over-the-counter medication. When I came out of that, I had enough money that I could do whatever I wanted. I began studies at Loyola Marymount in Los Angeles for a Masters in Pastoral Ministry, intending to do RCIA. However, I read about the priest shortage that year, and realized it would worsen. Naively, I thought the Church would use lay people as administrators. Upon the advice of a teacher, I moved to Berkeley to begin a Master of Divinity at the Franciscan School of Theology at the Graduate Theological Union. I wanted two things: 1) to test my vocation; 2) to be educated in the same program in which a priest would be prepared. This meant that I was very open about wanting to be a priest while at the Franciscan School. I did well in my studies, got good grades, especially in preaching and presiding, and loved every minute. I received a lot of affirmation from fellow students, from the parish where I did my field placement, and from a few very brave faculty and staff members. A wonderful and gracious musician, soon to become a priest himself, helped me set up and film my student mass. In 1999 I already knew I could do pastoral ministry. Upon graduation, with the entire student body loudly cheering, I knew I had been trained as a priest and had tested my vocation.

During the course of my theological studies, I learned that women had been ordained in the early church up to the 1200's. This made the refusal of the Roman Catholic Church to ordain women, or even to talk about it, perplexing to say the least. The job market for lay ministers had already begun to dry up in 1999. Even so, I took two more classes, both in Franciscan theology. I knew ordination wasn't going to happen any time soon, so I began to look around for another place to use my ministerial gifts. I decided to begin studies towards a doctorate in psychology, where I could use a priest's healing gifts.

The ordinations on the Danube in 2002 happened a few months before I began my doctoral studies. In the spring or summer of 2004, well into my doctoral studies, I learned that an ordination would be held in North America. After many attempts, I was able to contact Patricia Fresen, the director of the discernment program, and was finally accepted at the end of November for ordination in the summer of 2005. I decided to be ordained through this group (which later became known as *Roman Catholic Womenpriests* or *RCWP)* 1) because the Roman Catholic Church, in denial of its own history, still refuses to ordain women, 2) because the need among the people of the Church is very great, and 3) because there is clear apostolic succession of bishops in RCWP. With the huge support of my Corpus sacramental mentor, I was ordained a deacon in 2005 in Gananoque, Canada, and a priest in 2006 in Pittsburgh, Pennsylvania.

Ordination is an astounding process. My personal life has changed in ways I never imagined since ordination. It is as if I finally came to be more myself. I have grown and developed more fully in the areas where I knew I had a little talent. And new talents have shown up and developed as well. While I am not at all sure that I would say there is an "ontological" change at ordination, it is clear to me that God has been more present in my life since I said "Yes" to being ordained. And it seems to be clear to other people as well. I remain the normally imperfect person I was – but God seems to be able to work through me anyway.

The effects of ordination seem to have washed over into my psychotherapeutic vocation as well. I am finishing my psychology doctorate as this is written. More importantly, I am working in the field of psychology. I see adolescents in a continuation high school, and individuals in a very large community mental health clinic. I am beginning work in psychological assessment. I am very aware when God is in the room in my clinical work because what happens is an order above whatever native gifts I may have brought to psychology.

Being an irregular (as to the institution) Roman Catholic priest is a chancy thing. One never knows where one will be called to do ministry, indeed whether one will be able to do ministry at all. I was lucky enough to pair up with Victoria Rue and her mentor Don Cordero and his wife Juanita Cordero so that we were able to start masses in San Jose on the California State University campus. Now Juanita is also a priest; and we have a small community which meets for mass once a month in her home. Regrettably, Don, who was a great supporter of Roman Catholic Womenpriests, passed away in December 2007. As he wished, we continue on with our community – and they continue with Juanita and me.

I have presided on a few other occasions in Palo Alto and in Oakland. I am also an Assistant Program Coordinator for RCWP. In this capacity, I have been working with applicants and mentoring candidates for ordination to diaconate and then priesthood. It is an honor to work with these women and to be able to affirm their vocations. For some women, it is the first time anyone has affirmed their vocation to priesthood. This has been one of the greatest experiences of my priestly ministry.

Ordained a priest: 2006, Pittsburgh

CPSIA information can be obtained at www.ICGtesting.com
Printed in the USA
LVOW082307050412

276388LV00007B/64/P